MANAGERS, MARTIANS & MONSTERS

Seven vital lessons from classic thrillers that managers need

JONATHAN M. FREIMAN, Ph.D

Attribution &
Acknowledgement
of movie poster origins

The images are used for identification in the context of critical commentary of the work for which they serve as poster art, and metaphorically for totally unrelated chapter content. They make a significant contribution to the readers' understanding of the text, which could not practically be conveyed by words alone. The images are placed at the beginning of the chapter discussing the work to show the primary visual image associated with the work. Use for this purpose does not compete with the purposes of the original artwork, namely the creator providing graphic design services, and in turn the marketing of the promoted item.

These images are of posters, and the copyright for them is most likely owned by either the publisher or the creator of the work depicted. The owners of the copyrights may include MCA-Universal, Universal, Fox Video, 20th Century Fox, MGM/Turner, MGM/UA Entertainment, Turner/Warner Home Video, and Paramount/Viacom-Artisan. It is believed that the use of scaled-down, low-resolution images of posters to provide critical commentary on the film in question, not solely for illustration, qualifies as fair use under United States copyright law.

The copies are of sufficient resolution for commentary and identification but lower resolution than the original poster. Copies made from them will be of inferior quality, unsuitable as counterfeit artwork, pirate versions or for uses that would compete with the commercial purpose of the original artwork.

Dedication

To my mother and father, Gloria and Maurice, who made certain I was exposed to Shakespeare and Beethoven, but also knew the value of Roy Rogers and King Kong.

Contents

Prologue

I have always loved old movies, especially those sharing the science fiction, horror and supernatural genres. From the mid-1930s till the mid-1950s scores of mostly black and white thrillers delighted audiences across the globe. The names of featured actors read as a pantheon of silver screen legends—Bela Lugosi, Boris Karloff, Basil Rathbone, Lon Chaney, Jr., and many others graced the movies with their menacing presence.

Invariably, the films had compelling themes that drew the viewer in— *obsession* animated The Raven, the *lust for power* drove Tower of London, the *fear of alien possession* animated Invasion of the Body Snatchers, *mortal danger and supernatural contamination* impelled The Wolf Man, *seduction and betrayal* inspired The Picture of Dorian Gray, *self-deception* drove Forbidden Planet, and a *suicidal inertia* within governments and large institutions was the force behind The Day The Earth Stood Still.

My career has been spent in large manufacturing corporations such as General Motors, Boeing and Goodrich in both production and human resource management. In this book I sought to combine a vocation and avocation into an entertaining learning experience.

While teaching a class in performance management to a group of supervisors, I used The Raven as a bizarre example of the power of expectations. The way they were intrigued—the way their attention was focused as never before—energized and encouraged me to pursue this work.

My fondest wish is that you find this book entertaining and informative, and that it encourages you to see these old classics if they've escaped you, or revisit them for another look at some of our old friends.

JMF

Chapter 1
The Power of Expectations—
The Raven

The pendulum was his pride and joy. After laboring at great expense to replicate many of Poe's instruments of torture, none satisfied so much as the great swinging blade. The elegant, hypnotic arc it described as it hissed through the air was a thing of beauty only to be matched by its return flight. With each cycle the whirring of finely meshed gears and precision bearings would bring the oily breath of the heavy razor-edged steel a fraction closer to the granite altar upon which its bound victim could witness its inevitable descent.

Dr. Richard Vollin, a retired surgeon of obsessive tendencies, believed that by projecting and manifesting his expectations onto others he could avenge the torture of his scorned, unrequited infatuation with a beautiful female patient—by torturing those who tortured him. That Vollin was a lovesick madman is undeniable, but had he nonetheless expressed some deeper understanding of human motivation that was not at all deranged? The 1935 horror classic,

The Raven, asks the same question as has been pondered in such diverse venues as education, science, business and sports.

A Hideous Expectation is Born:
The Experiments Begin

A terrible car accident severely injures the daughter of a prominent judge, and as her life ebbs away he's informed that only one surgeon has the skill to perform the delicate operation she needs. Judge Thatcher rushes to Dr. Vollin's (Bela Lugosi's) home to implore him but Vollin refuses until he learns the other physicians had acknowledged his superior capabilities. His ego thus assuaged, he agrees to come out of retirement.

The operation is a complete success and Vollin, doting upon his mending patient, confuses gratitude with affection and becomes infatuated with lovely, but engaged, Jean Thatcher. Her father senses this preoccupation and tries to steer Vollin away from his daughter, but the doctor is infuriated with this attempt and threatens revenge. The two part on uneasy terms.

The next evening a rapping at his mansion's door brought not a "stately raven" but the escaped convict Edmund Bateman. Bateman (Boris Karloff) has sought out Vollin to ask him to change his appearance in order to avoid capture. Again, Vollin declines, but when Bateman shares childhood recollections of the severe taunting he received because he was considered ugly, and the meanness he felt towards others as a result, Vollin's imagination is triggered and he agrees to operate.

The doctor reasons that if ugly people do ugly things, there would be no limit to the acts a truly hideous individual could perform. If his expectations were correct, Bateman would be the henchman he needed to carry out his revenge. The surgery is performed and Bateman emerges disfigured. Thereafter, Vollin enjoys almost complete control of Bateman as only he can restore him to normal.

In the real world evidence for the influence of expectations upon performance has long been sought. The classic Oak School experiment, carried out in the mid-1960s by Robert Rosenthal and Lenore Jacobson, provided some compelling observations. Twenty percent of 650 elementary school students were identified as having high intellectual potential from the results of a standardized achievement test. This information was shared with their teachers.

At year's end the children were again tested and those earlier identified as most promising showed the most growth. There was just one problem. *The children identified as having high intellectual potential were selected by means of a random number table. The only difference between them and the rest of the student population was in the minds of the teachers!* The teachers' expectations, and the way those expectations manifested themselves, made all the difference.

This same experiment was replicated in a laboratory using rats and technicians. Again the "specially bred" rats were identified, and the techs were asked to train them to move through a maze and find food as quickly as possible. The results were as before—the rats were identical in ability but their performance differed because of their tech's expectations. In fact, the techs found the "gifted" rats far more personable as well.

Additional animal experimentation with Norwegian Warf Rats at Johns Hopkins University Medical School once again added to the field. The famous Dr. Curt P. Richter performed a series of experiments in the Psychobiological Laboratory during the late 1950's, ostensibly seeking to understand the phenomenon of sudden death in laboratory animals.

One of the experiments consisted of dropping individual rats into water-filled glass swimming jars and timing their endurance. Some rats were wild and others were specially bred for the laboratory. Counterintuitively, the wild rats often died within two minutes, while their domestic brethren often swam 40 to 60 hours. Richter reasoned the frequent handling the specially bred rats experienced somehow better prepared them for the water endurance trial, as some of the wild rats died suddenly when in the grasp of the researcher, apparently from shock.

He attempted to provide that same sort of conditioning to the wild specimens by repeatedly lifting the immersed rats from the swimming jars for brief periods. The rats' expectations of rescue soared. Afterwards, the wild rats swam as long, or longer than their city cousins. Richter concluded that once the *hopelessness* of their situation was eliminated, the rats again became aggressive, tried to escape, and reach their now achievable objective of survival.

A Strange Type of Hospitality:
Changing Expectations at the Firm

The design for Dr. Vollin's revenge was never in doubt, but he needed a pretext to lure the victims into his trap. He invites Judge Thatcher, his daughter Jean, her fiancée and two other couples to spend the weekend at his home. The judge disapproves but acquiesces at his daughter's insistence.

Frivolous parlor games following dinner the first night are punctuated by Vollin's fireside discourse on Edgar Allan Poe and their mutual fascination with torture and death. The guests find the discussion unsettling and all agree to retire to their warm rooms on this storm-tossed night.

At 11 p.m. Bateman, posing as Vollin's servant, forces Judge Thatcher down into the cavernous, vaulted basement where Poe's devices were replicated. He is shackled to the slab under the pendulum, and at Vollin's command the great blade is put in motion.

Employee expectations were a major barrier for CEO Eric Schmidt as he tried to change the disastrous course Novell was on when he took command in 1997. The Provo, Utah software firm was dominant in LAN (Local Area Network) technology shortly after its founding in 1983, but a series of bad acquisitions and unsuccessful products in the mid-1990s made it look like Novell was doomed.

Schmidt, coming from Sun Microsystems, made a series of rapid changes designed to signal the beginning of a new regime as well as have a business impact. Most of executive management was replaced and 1,000 employees were removed from the rolls. Layers of management were reduced from seven to four and cost-cutting measures were introduced. The most difficult challenges he faced though, were keeping key talent and changing the fearfulness he detected.

In a series of fact-to-face meetings with some of the company's most talented people he learned that many were demoralized, for they had no expectation of being listened to, and had decided to remain silent and keep a low profile. Some of the best ideas were being lost. Novell's "culture of fear" as Schmidt characterized it, was not unusual for firms in trouble. People were worried and did not want to complain and be targeted for layoff. They just agreed, at least superficially, with upper management's proposals, signaling agreement with what was coined the "Novell nod."

Schmidt showed the employees that he understood the cultural problems and was committed to fixing them. He established a new recognition system and instituted a new incentive system that paid a 100% bonus at the end of each quarter for meeting all objectives. His emphasis on personal communication gained traction and he continued to hold frequent, small meetings to build trust and stay close to the people. Novell's turnover rate plunged to 15%, well below the industry average 22%, and profits rose to $192 million in 1999 after a loss of $78 million two years earlier. From being ignored and unappreciated to being recognized and rewarded, the expectations of Novell's employees had been dramatically shifted.

At Ford, Alan Mulally faced a challenge of even greater magnitude. In 2006, the year he took over as president and CEO, the historic auto giant lost $12.7 billion. His reception by the existing hierarchy was reserved. Having spent almost forty years at Boeing, Mulally was first confronted by the skeptical Ford executive staff. They had grave doubts about his ability to comprehend their complex and unfamiliar business. He answered famously, "An automobile has about 10,000 moving parts, right? An airplane has two million, and it has to stay up in the air."

Mulally quickly assessed the culture as dysfunctional and defeatist by nature, with a propensity for accepting mediocrity as the norm. Managers were more concerned about their careers than about customers. Information was rarely shared between divisions. Executives were rotated into new assignments every two years regardless of merit or mastery of their current assignments. Side conversations were common in meetings and executives often sent substitutes rather than attend in person. Mulally was about to create a new "normal."

He increased the frequency of staff meetings from monthly to weekly and attendance was mandatory—no substitutions. Division Chiefs were encouraged to bring a different subordinate each time for the purposes of development and communication. Executives were expected to know the key details of their operations without referring to their notes or assistants. The Black Berry was banned as were side conversations—the person speaking could expect the undivided attention of all. Failures as well as successes became part of the agenda. If an executive mentioned a problem, others were expected to assist in the solution. Mulally halted all automatic rotations, and promotions became merit-based. These things were unheard of at Ford.

Ford divested itself of Jaguar, Land Rover and Aston Martin as part of a strategy designed to focus on core products. It was the only U.S. automaker that did not need a federal bailout or go through bankruptcy court in 2009. 2011 was the second most profitable in the company's 109-year history with earnings reaching $6.1 billion. Additionally, Consumer Reports rated Ford's reliability equal to their best Japanese rivals. Mulally instituted a fundamental change in the behaviors of his top executives by communicating and enforcing a new set of rigorous expectations that resulted in a dramatic improvement in business performance.

Expectations at Work:
Performance Management Do's and Don'ts

The annual performance management cycle provides an excellent opportunity for establishing and reviewing expectations for achievement and behavior. Below are several important points.

DO:

- Link objective to overall business strategy.
- Show employees how they fit into the plan.
- Reach mutual agreement—get commitment.
- Make objectives difficult but attainable.
- Stress clarity. Objectives must be explicit.
- Express confidence to employees of positive outcome.
- Show interest and support—follow up.
- Offer help and resources, if necessary.
- Plan a series of small victories/successes for apprehensive employees.
- Communicate high expectations through words and actions.
- Recognize and be aware you are subject to biases when making judgments.

DON'T:

- Fail to get buy-in from employees, line and senior management regarding assessment system.
- Place much emphasis upon evaluations made by appraisers who know employees for less than one year. Forms should indicate time known.
- Use single appraiser if at all possible. Use multiple raters, and if from peer group, average the scores.
- Give score for overall performance before rating on 10-15 job factors. Rater will have better frame of reference if component factors are rated prior to overall score.
- Underestimate impact of expectations expressed to new hires. These are especially important and future performance and career progress can be greatly affected.
- Attempt to conceal feelings from subordinates. A manager who believes an employee will perform poorly communicates that message without conscious action. Instead, work on a performance improvement plan.
- Assume employees understand that a problem exists.
- Assume employees know what has to be done.
- Fail to acknowledge when a problem is corrected.
- Pair your new hires and/or recent graduates with "old pro" first-line supervisors who have been judged lacking competence for higher levels, or new and inexperienced first-lines. Rather pair them with experienced middle managers or upper level executives to avoid feelings of abandonment, provide visibility of new talent to key decision makers, and build future relationships.

A Pressing Engagement:
Expectations on Ice

The bedroom Jean Thatcher occupies is lowered, by means of fantastic hydraulics, down into the fathomless dungeon where her father is already beneath the pendulum. She begs Bateman to spare her but he responds that he must obey Vollin to have any chance for a normal appearance. She swears that others are capable of undoing the damage and help will be provided—if only he helps her. For a moment he seems torn.

A windowless room, where the walls converge slowly with tremendous force, is another Poe invention the maddened Vollin has planned to use for his revenge. At pistol point he orders Jean and her fiancée into the room together. With the toss of a lever the room is sealed and the walls activated. Bateman asks Vollin if she is to die. "Yes."

As the crushing walls close in on the betrothed couple Vollin tells Bateman that he has done nobly and will now restore his face. Bateman weighs the value of his own fate against the girl's life and decides on the side of the angels. Despite being warned he throws the lever to stop the walls and release the couple. Vollin fires his pistol once, mortally wounding him. Jean and her fiancée rush from the murderous room as the dying Bateman charges Vollin, knocking him to the ground and dragging him semiconscious into that same room. With his last effort he throws the lever once again and Vollin is destroyed by his own instrument of torture and the folly of false expectations.

The 1980 Winter Olympic Games in Lake Placid, NY pitted the youngest hockey team the United States ever fielded against a dominant and profession-al Soviet team. In the last four Olympics before the 1980 games, the Russians were 27-1-1 (won, tied, lost) against all opponents and had outscored them 175-44. Since the U.S. had last beaten the Russians twenty years earlier they had won every gold medal, yet the role expectations played in this match would be as important as skill, strategy and endurance.

Thirteen days before the historic meeting at the Olympic Field House the two teams met for an exhibition game at Madison Square Garden in New York City. Herb Brooks, the Machiavellian head coach of the Americans, placed no stress on his players and uncharacteristically told them to just go out and have fun. He allowed his best goalie to play for only half the game to ensure the Russians didn't get a good look at what was coming their way. The Americans were in awe of the skill and speed the Russians displayed and hardly felt worthy of being on the same ice. The Russians won 10-3. A year earlier at the Garden, the Russians beat the best of the NHL 6-0.

Play began February 12th and the Russians beat Japan and Holland with a combined score of 33-4. The USA tied Sweden 2-2, and then beat the Czechs 7-3, scoring five times in twenty-six minutes. Norway and Romania then fell to the Americans, and West Germany, though putting up a tough struggle, was defeated 4-2. The Russians won matches against Finland and Canada. The main event was next.

The Americans initially had no expectations for the outcome, nor were they burdened by them. All they anticipated was a tough match against professionals, to hold together as a team, and to be tested to the limit. The Russians expected to face the same team they had roundly defeated thirteen days earlier.

The Russians were the first to score in the opening twenty-minute period, but the Americans answered with one of their own. The Russians scored again, and with one second left, as the Russians were preparing to leave the ice with a 2-1 lead, the Americans slammed a puck into the Russian goal and tied it 2-2. The Americans were ready. Their expectations were changing. Coach Brooks told his twenty-man team, "You were born to be players. You were meant to be here. This moment is yours!" The youngest hockey team the USA had ever put together—18 of 20 still in college—was skating with the best.

The Americans scored no goals in the second of three periods and the Russians pulled ahead 3-2. Eight and one-half minutes into the third and final period the Americans tied the game 3-3. The Americans were determined. Ninety seconds later the American team scored again and led 4-3 with ten minutes left in the match. That was the first lead for Americans over Russians in an Olympic hockey game in twenty years. This was no time for the Americans to relax however, for the Russians had scored four times in 15 minutes against the Canadians and won 6-4. The Russians tried furiously to score, but the American coaches had reduced the skating time of their players to 35 seconds per shift (from the standard 45 seconds), and they had fresher legs—and a more determined spirit. They could taste victory. A horn blast reverberated throughout the stadium. Game over, Friday evening, 7:26 p.m., February 22, 1980. The crowd erupted in delirious celebration.

Afterwards Sergei Makarov, one of the Russian players, would remark at the difference between this and the team they had played thirteen days earlier, "Their eyes were bright," he said in a heavy accent. "Their eyes were burning. It was team."

The Russian head coach, Viktor Tikhonov said, "No matter what we tried we could not get that 10-3 game out of the players' minds. The players told me it would be no problem. It turned out to be a very big problem."

Taken in the context of an America enduring the Iranian hostage crisis, the Soviet invasion of Afghanistan, soaring inflation, high unemployment and a sense that the nation had lost its way, the victory on that cold winter night signaled a resurgence Americans longed to feel.

The power of expectations is undeniable, but it is a force in need of direction. When expectations are well formed, realistic and focused, they can provide motivation that induces people to reach beyond themselves and achieve greatness. When expectations are based upon giddy fantasies fueled by wishful thinking, they can result in disaster and dismay, leaving in their wake the crestfallen and defeated. Dr. Vollin and the Russians would concur.

References

Biron, Michal, Elaine Farndale, et al. "Performance management effectiveness: lessons from world-leading firms." *International Journal of Human Resource Management*. Vol. 22. No. 6 (2011): 1294–1311.

Coffey, Wayne. *The Boys of Winter*. 1st ed. New York: Three Rivers Press, 2005.

Friedlander, Louis, dir. *The Raven*. Perf. Bela Logosi, and Boris Karloff. 1935. Film.

Fryer, Bronwyn . "Leading Through Rough Times: An Interview with Novell's Eric Schmidt." *Harvard Business Review*. May 2001: 117-123.

Kiley, David. "Ford's Savior?." *Business Week*. 16 Mar 2009: 31-34.

Kiley, David. "The New Heat On Ford." *Business Week*. 4 Jun 2007: 33-38.

Livingston, J. Sterling. "Pygmalion in management." *Harvard Business Review*. Jul 1969: 81-89.

Miller, Corey E. "How Accurate Are Your Performance Appraisals?" *Public Personnel Management*. Vol. 35 .Issue 2 (2006): p153-162.

Naughton, Keith. "The Happiest Man in Detroit." *Business Week*. 7 Feb 2011: 66-71.

Richter, Curt P. "On the Phenomenon of Sudden Death in Animals and Man." *Psychosomatic Medicine*. 19.3 (1957): 191-198.

Rosenthal, Robert, and Lenore Jacobsen. *Pygmalion In The Classroom*. New York: Holt, Rinehart and Winston, Inc., 1968.

WALTER PIDGEON
ANNE FRANCIS
LESLIE NIELSEN
FORBIDDEN PLANET

Chapter 2
Narcissism at Work—
Forbidden Planet

On the fourth planet from the main sequence star Altair, an ancient and extinct alien civilization has left behind a mysterious, subterranean machine that has maintained itself in perfect operating order for two thousand centuries. In the year 2257, a United Planets Cruiser traveling at over sixteen times the speed of light reaches Altair 4 to discover the fate of a scientific expedition launched twenty years earlier. Only three of the original thirteen escaped being murdered by a malignant and invisible force.

Dr. Edward Morbius and his daughter Altaira are the sole survivors, believing themselves apparently immune to whatever killed the others. With the exception of his wife, who died of natural causes, seven of the ten victims were literally torn limb from limb. The remaining three were vaporized with their ship as they tried to takeoff and return to Earth. Morbius expresses his fear that the crew will experience a similar fate and urges them to leave.

For the past two decades Dr. Morbius has patiently and methodically studied the language, civilization and advanced science of the Krell. By use of a Krell "plastic educator" he was able, at great risk to himself, to permanently double his intelligence. Even with his enhanced capabilities however, a deep character flaw prevents Morbius from the insight needed to understand the reason for the murders and the directing force behind them. Dr. Morbius is a narcissist.

In the 1956 science fiction classic *Forbidden Planet*, Dr. Morbius (portrayed by Walter Pidgeon and supported by Anne Francis as his daughter and Leslie Nielsen as the able Captain J.J. Adams), demonstrates the wide spectrum of both positive and negative behaviors that those with narcissistic tendencies can evidence.

In Greek mythology Narcissus was the son of the river god Cephissus and the nymph Leiriope; he was distinguished for his beauty. His mother was told that he would have a long life, provided he never looked upon his own features. His rejection, however, of the love of the nymph Echo or of his lover Ameinias drew upon him the vengeance of the gods. He fell in love with his own reflection in the waters of a spring and pined away. The flower that bears his name, also called a Daffodil, sprang up where he died.

As a psychological condition, a narcissist's ego will reveal high levels of self-esteem, grandiosity, self-focus, and self-importance. They think they are more physically attractive and intelligent than just about everyone, and would rather be admired than liked. Narcissists are not just found on remote planetary systems, but rather often in places of work as bosses, peers and subordinates. They can be brilliant leaders and are found in the upper levels of many organizations. How may we best draw upon their strengths and compensate for their weaknesses?

Identifying the Narcissist:
Five Trait Clusters

1. <u>Charismatic, Charming and Dramatic</u>

Dr. Morbius is a striking figure—Dark, penetrating eyes flash from a noble brow crowned with jet-black hair. His moustache and beard are meticulously trimmed and the whole gives his face the air of a sorcerer or mystic. He adorns himself entirely in black and completes his imposing presence with a resonant baritone.

While at first reluctant to receive visitors, he soon becomes a congenial host to the ship's officers with the help of his adoring daughter and Robby the Robot. Alta idolizes her father, ignores his faults, magnifies his strengths and sees him as nearly infallible.

Earth's history is replete with individuals who understood the value of a dramatic presence as well. A pure white Norman horse named Intendant was favored by Napoleon. He was mainly used for parades and reviews because of his calm, steady, and graceful nature, but his stunning impact was not overlooked by the great general. Similarly, George Washington always brought along one or two white parade horses when traveling. More recently, the ivory handled Colts of General Patton (who practiced his scowls in a mirror), and the aviator-styled sunglasses and corncob pipe of General Macarthur served similar purposes. In industry, the self-styled John Z. DeLorean, one of GM's youngest and most flamboyant vice presidents, had plastic surgery to enhance his jaw line while in his early 40s. Narcissists are very image conscious and believe they are more physically attractive than reality would confirm.

2. Passionate, Isolated and a Voracious Study

Dr. Morbius has studied Krell science for twenty years in complete isolation. As a trained philologist or linguist, he has been able to decipher some small parts of this huge treasure. He built Robby by himself, something he likens to a task a Krell child would be assigned, and wisely endows the robot with an absolute inhibition against harming humans.

Morbius describes the Krell as an "almost divine race" which mysteriously, on the eve of possibly their greatest scientific achievement, were destroyed in a single night. He provides a grand tour of the Krell wonders to the captain and his first officer. The astounding scale of Krell engineering is displayed in the subterranean machine which is forty miles wide, contains 7,800 separate levels and is powered by 9,200 thermonuclear reactors working in tandem fifty miles beneath the surface. They inquire as to the actual purpose of the machine, but Dr. Morbius is evasive.

DeLorean also had a scholarly bent like Morbius. Born in 1925, he attended Detroit's public grade schools, excelled at a technical high school, was awarded a scholarship at Lawrence Technical University and was elected to the school's honor society. Afterwards he attended the Chrysler Institute of Engineering and graduated with a Master's Degree in 1952. By 1957 he had his MBA from the University of Michigan.

DeLorean joined Pontiac Division of General Motors in 1954, became division chief engineer seven years later, introduced the legendary Pontiac GTO in 1964, and was promoted to division head the following year at age 40. He had finally made it to the hallowed 14th floor at GM's headquarters where the executive offices were located. There was only one problem—he was a was a poor fit.

Narcissists are not good team players. They want all the credit for things that go well (as he received for the GTO), and team membership generally entails a form of sharing credit and blame. They don't necessarily try to fit in with their peer group, nor be liked and have friends. They also want to be the center of attention, and in the respectful ambiance of the board room DeLorean felt suffocated. He left GM in 1973 to start his own car company, which began manufacturing the *DeLorean* in 1981, and closed less than two years later. Though esthetically pleasing, the car lacked the engine and running gear of a true sports car and was never accepted by the motoring press or public. He did achieve a type of immortality though, for the car was featured in the popular *Back To The Future* movie series, and he was very happy for that.

3. Devalues and Exploits Without Remorse

Morbius has only his daughter for companionship. Altaira has him, Robby, and some domesticated animals for company. He has deceived her about Earth and made it a dangerous and unattractive place in her mind. She has no desire to go there, and he shows no concern for this young lady's normal social development. She is happily marooned by virtue of his deceptions, but both Morbius and his daughter genuinely love living on Altair 4.

The ability to devalue and exploit people is both a strength and a weakness to narcissists. In positions of leadership this trait may make it easier for them to reach the hard decisions: to sell or close a business, or layoff thousands. Narcissists will not agonize for inordinate periods nor cause costly delays as matters of conscience.

For example, under the leadership of Bill Gates, Microsoft agreed to a $97 million settlement to cover more than 8,000 employees who suffered financial damage from being wrongly classified as contract employees and denied standard benefits and stock purchase opportunities. Their work assignments and working conditions were virtually indistinguishable from full-time employees, yet their pay and benefits after years of service were in no way comparable.

Narcissists crave to be understood, but it is a one-way street as they lack empathy for others. They are often unlikable and find intimacy difficult. They would rather lecture and indoctrinate than allow their world-view to be challenged. Developing subordinates is not a strength, for a successful underling is a threat, not a potential successor for the business. Learning from others does not come easily to them; they want to be surrounded by yes-men and very few can stand even well meaning opposition. Independent-minded managers cannot last very long, as DeLorean at GM demonstrates, for while DeLorean himself was a narcissist, the top corporate leaders at GM were similar and spawned a culture that typically excluded managers capable of critical thinking and analysis in favor of "team players." The result was that those allowed closest to the inner workings and key decisions of the corporation were also those least able to appreciate what they were witnessing.

4. <u>Over Controlling and Grandiose</u>

Dr. Morbius has determined he will be the sole arbiter of all Krell scientific knowledge. When Captain Adams asserts that this discovery is too big for any one man to manage, Morbius launches into a tirade:

> I have come to the unalterable conclusion that man is unfit, as yet, to receive such knowledge, such almost limitless power.... Such portions of the Krell science as I may, from time to time, deem

suitable and safe I shall dispense to Earth. Other portions I shall withhold, and in this I shall be answerable exclusively to my own conscience and judgment.

Dr. Morbius seeks and will fight for complete control of this remarkable find. Allotments of Krell knowledge to Earth will be as the fancy strikes him, and all accolades shall accrue to him.

When fantasies of unlimited control, success and brilliance are challenged, dramatic narcissists can experience tremendous anger and become vindictive. In the workplace, a narcissistic CEO can create a climate of fearful and unquestioning subordination. While a brilliant entrepreneur, Steve Jobs of Apple was famous for publicly humiliating staff members. Hewlett Packard CEO Carly Fiorina became sullen when argued with, and Maine Senator Ed Muskie was known for his explosive temper.

Consider the archetypical automobile magnate Henry Ford as an example of the control mentality. In the face of a horrendous turnover rate of 370%, on January 5, 1914 Henry Ford's Five Dollar Day plan was announced in Highland Park, Michigan. The heart of this revolutionary plan was a profit-sharing program that would increase the minimum daily wage of *qualified* workers to five dollars. The average prevailing daily wage was $2.34 at the time. Ten thousand men gathered at the plant entrance the following day.

To implement this plan Ford established the Sociological Department. Made up of some of Ford's most trusted employees, it was charged with determining which workers were eligible to participate. The department sent investigators into all of the workers' homes to observe how they were living and ask probing questions about alcohol use, marital relations, and spending habits. They were looking for evidence of thrift, cleanliness, sobriety, family values, and good morals in general. The workers tolerated this intrusiveness for the sake of the wage, and turnover dropped to 16% in 1915.

By 1932 the wage had been reduced to $4.00 per day due to falling sales and the Great Depression. Control was maintained by other means afterwards, as Ford employed company police and labor spies to prevent unionization. A narcissist in control is a happy narcissist.

Narcissistic personality disorder (NPD) was the diagnosis for an Australian man named Omar Jihad Yusuf in 2005. He drove a Ferrari, purchased a racehorse, and enjoyed a thoroughly affluent life until an investigation brought him down. He adopted the title of "Prince," saying the Saudi royal family had bestowed it upon him, and falsely claimed to have interests in pharmaceuticals, oil, aviation, property and perfume employing 6,500 people worldwide with annual revenues of $650 million.

The funding for his lifestyle came from 109 investors who were defrauded of $7.29 million as they invested in his fictitious trucking company on the promise of very attractive returns. Upon being exposed he fled to Malaysia and continued burning through his victims' funds until being charged with fraud and returned to Australia. His lawyer claimed that others contributed to his delusions of grandeur.

Narcissists believe that they are entitled to more positive outcomes in life than others and are fixated on issues of power, beauty, status, prestige and superiority. This is often done to compensate for a very fragile sense of self-esteem.

5. Arrogance, Conceit and Low Self-Knowledge

While Dr. Morbius is dozing in the Krell laboratory the invisible force attacks the captain's United Planets Cruiser and crew at its landing site, killing one. The ship's main defenses are brought to bear, and while being bombarded by three billion electron volts in a searing ray attack, the creature blazes into incandescence and reveals a truly hideous form. Morbius rouses from his slumber and the creature fades to nothingness. The giant Krell machine falls silent after displaying furious activity on its output gauges moments earlier.

Captain Adams and his first officer, Doc Ostrow, rush back to Morbius'dwelling to confront him. As the captain questions Morbius, Doc Ostrow slips into the Krell laboratory and applies the brain boosting "plastic educator" to himself. The boost has lethal consequences for the Doc, but before he expires informs Adams of the insights he's gained from his expanded intelligence, which now exceeds that of Morbius. The giant Krell machine was designed to enable "civilization without instrumentality" or the ability for every Krell to project any type of force or matter to any part of the planet by mere thought alone. If they wanted something, they could wish it into existence with the help of the big machine.

The Krell overlooked one thing though--the savage primitive from which they evolved. When the machine was activated it obeyed not only their conscious thoughts but also the wishes of their uncontrolled subconscious. In one fateful night the machine brought into being all the rapaciousness, all the fearfulness, all the jealousies and prejudices and base desires that their civilization had suppressed for millennia and let them loose in the wholesale slaughter of a planet.

Morbius reacts to the death of Ostrow unsympathetically, "The fool, the meddling idiot. As though his ape's brain could contain the secrets of the Krell!"

Suddenly, Robby detects an intruder approaching. Morbius orders the robot to stop it by any means necessary, but Robby freezes and is unable to act. Captain Adams concludes that what is approaching them is a monstrous force generated by the Krell machine as directed by the mind of Morbius, and that Robby could not act due to his absolute inhibition against harming humans. Morbius denies that possibility, for the last Krell died 2,000 centuries ago and only they could communicate with the machine. Adams asserts that since his mind was artificially boosted, the Krell machine has identified him as a Krell and was abiding by his wishes.

Morbius, with growing horror, finally gains insight into his own mind and realizes he was responsible for the deaths of the other members of the expeditionary party. Once they sought to leave Altair 4 his subconscious viewed them as enemies and sent a monster of energy to destroy them. He is doing so once again against Adams and his crew, but this time there is a difference. Altaira is in love with Adams and is now about to share his fate. The three of them dash into the Krell laboratory and hide behind a wall of Krell metal 26" thick.

No less high-minded were the aspirations of Volvo's chairman, Pehr G. Gyllenhammar when he opened the new Uddevalla assembly plant in 1988. His goal was to humanize automobile manufacturing by using small teams of highly trained workers to build entire cars and eliminate the tedium of the assembly line. Ignoring the advice of operations management experts and line executives, he was convinced his system could compete internationally and have the added benefit of reducing absenteeism and turnover. He was wrong.

On old-fashioned assembly lines, workers complete relatively simple tasks generally lasting 30 seconds to three minutes on a paced line. At Uddevalla, a team of workers typically spend two to three hours on one car. While turnover plunged to 5 percent from 16, output figures never reached world-class levels. An MIT report in 1990 concluded that while the leading Japanese-style lean-production plant it studied needed only 13.3 hours to weld, paint and assemble a car slightly smaller than the large luxury cars made at Uddevalla, the Volvo plant required about 50 hours, *excluding welding and painting.*

Another example might be Ray Noorda, CEO of the software company Novell, who wanted to challenge Microsoft's dominance of the business office environment and, against the advice of investors, purchased WordPerfect for $1.4 billion in 1994. Two years later it was sold for $124 million, less than 10% of the price paid. Noorda is no longer with Novell.

When a narcissist is presented with some hard life lessons that take him down a peg or two, real change is possible. This can include the loss of an important relationship, a huge career setback, or major financial damage. He is left with his own thoughts or demons, and has no one to blame but himself.

How To Work With A Narcissist:
Useful Do's and Don'ts

Narcissists can be challenging to work with, but because of the ubiquity of the type, there is little possibility that they can be avoided indefinitely. The following are tips that might prove useful.

Don't gossip with them. They might take the tidbit you shared right back to the person being discussed. If they can use it to their advantage, they will.

Don't borrow from them or lend to them. If you borrow something from a narcissist they are being provided with leverage over you. You owe them and they will exploit that indebtedness. They are also poor at returning what they've borrowed, and will sometimes look upon the object as a gift. It's all about them.

Don't criticize or point out mistakes. Especially if you are in a reporting relationship to this person, but even otherwise, it will be viewed as an attack, not a helpful correction. If you must, use the utmost tact in private and always make it sound like a mild suggestion. If you can guide them into making the discovery for themselves, so much the better.

Don't challenge their power, authority, or greatness. Truly "legends in their own minds," the sensitivity of a narcissist to real or imagined slights, confrontations, or mutinies is beyond measure. It will long be remembered, never forgiven and entitle you to a cherished place on their enemies list.

Don't boast or brag about yourself. While they rarely see themselves as proud or vain, narcissists readily, perhaps gleefully, detect those qualities in others. You will make yourself into a threat or competitor in their eyes. If they are in supervisory positions, you will seem less in need or deserving of a reward, i.e., a promotion or raise. Step away from the red flag.

Don't confide in them. Remember their lack of empathy. Though some may be able to feign compassion, in reality you are providing them with an arsenal to use against you. The special relationship you hope to conjure through the sharing of personal information will not be reciprocated.

Don't share ideas with them. Narcissists will happily claim your ideas or your work as their own. The only safe way to share an idea with them is in writing, preferably with copies to yourself and others.

Don't try to reason with them if they are in a narcissistic rage. If they indulge themselves in a tantrum, it is time to back away. It will pass. Speak softly to them and take your leave. Alternatively, you may want to suggest that they take a well-deserved break—even just to walk around the parking lot.

Do get written instructions whenever possible. Narcissists, especially in leadership positions, are often so absorbed and passionate that they may not remember what they have asked others to do. When presented with the completed work, they may reject it outright or severely criticize it, for they may have forgotten what they originally requested. Protect yourself.

Do show respect and admiration. Narcissists can be high achievers and create wealth and employment for many. A sincere expression of appreciation will always be well received. Do not, however, try to be manipulative. A fawning subordinate trying to gain favor through flattery will be found out.

Do change positions. If you are in a larger firm and transfer opportunities exist, take advantage of them. If your supervisor is a narcissist, your chances of being developed for high office are reduced, perhaps nil. Then again, your supervisor can be brilliant at what he does and learning from him might make the rest bearable. Does he have coattails worth riding?

Do seek a go-between. If the relationship is genuinely troubled, seeking the aid of an intermediary can be beneficial. This person can either teach you how to deal with the narcissist or actually act as a neutral who has safe passage between the parties.

Do use the 360-feedback tool. This popular feedback tool enables anonymous inputs from an individual's peers, subordinates and supervisor. It is especially useful when working with difficult people who are generally resistant to criticism and become quite defensive. Employing a consulting psychologist to help interpret the information can make the news easier to receive. The narcissist will be flattered that the organization would hire a professional for this purpose and view it as confirmation of his own importance.

Do over-communicate. Provide plenty of information to the narcissist. Never surprise him. Keep him posted on your activities. If the information flow is excessive, he will tell you. A dearth of information can lead to unfounded suspicions.

Do use humor and sarcasm. In a peer relationship, a lighthearted approach can work. Humor can be a valuable tool to restore perspective and reduce tension. Always remember that in humor there is the risk of misinterpretation, so know your audience well. That is especially true if you are daring enough to apply this to your supervisor.

No such contrivances were attempted with Dr. Morbius. Captain Adams and his crew artlessly chose direct confrontation and insult as their tools. The reaction was predictable and the monster was summoned forth. Were there, however, alternative approaches?

How would Morbius have reacted if:

- They had heaped praise upon the doctor for his painstaking work and amazing discoveries?

- Worked through Altaira as an intermediary?
- Placed him in contact with high officials on Earth and offered him a position as leader of a vast research team of his own choosing?
- Or had Altaira professed her undying love for her father, but compared her love for the captain to the one he had for her mother?

The story unfolds to its inexorable conclusion. Unable to stop this monster from his own subconscious, the doctor, his daughter and the captain retreat to the safety of the Krell laboratory. Their redoubt shields them with walls made of incredibly dense Krell metal over two feet thick.

The giant Krell engine rises to the task and supplies the monster with all the energy it needs to defeat the armor. Gauges in the laboratory display an almost infinite amount of output as the Krell metal shows the first signs of warming. Seconds pass and the metal glows a dull red, then brighter still until it approaches the white heat of refractory temperatures and slowly turns molten.

Morbius confronts his own evil self and is stricken. In his dying moments he instructs the captain to overload the great Krell nuclear reactors and bring about the destruction of the planet. The captain and Altaira flee to the ship and escape to a safe distance.

Dr. Morbius, the brilliant narcissist, could not save himself nor be saved by others. The intelligence and talent that was lost need not be lost to us if we can understand this very difficult, yet very valuable type of individual.

Captain Adams commiserates with Altaira:

> Alta, about a million years from now the human race will have crawled up to where the Krell stood in their great moment of triumph and tragedy. And your father's name will shine again like a beacon in the galaxy....

References

Campbell, Keith W., et al. "Narcissism, Confidence, and Risk Attitude." *Journal of Behavioral Decision Making.* 17. (2004): 297-311.

De Vries, Manfred F. R. "The Leadership Mystique." *Academy of Management Executive.* 8.3 (1994): 73-89.

De Vries, Manfred F. R., and Danny Miller. "Personality, Culture, and Organization." *Academy of Management Review.* 11.2 (1986): 266-79.

Hagan, Kate. "'Prince' of Broadmeadows defrauded 109 investors and lived the high life." *Age* [Melbourne] 11 Jul 2008, First ed. 5.

Kramer, Roderick. "The Great Intimidators." *Harvard Business Review.* Feb 2006: 88-96.

Lavender, Neil, and Alan Cavaiola. *The One-Way Relationship Workbook.* Oakland, CA: New Harbinger Publications, 2010.

Maccoby, Michael. *Narcissistic Leaders.* New York: Random House, 2003.

Ranft, Annette, and Hugh O'Neill. "Board composition and high-flying founders: Hints of trouble to come?." *Academy ol Management Executive.* 15.1 (2001): 126-138.

Schwartz, Howard S. "Narcissism Project and Corporate Decay: The Case of General Motors." *Business Ethics Quarterly.* 1.3 (1991): 249-68.

Useem, Jerry. "1914: Ford offers $5 a day." *Fortune.* 27 Jun 2005.

Wilcox, Fred M., dir. *Forbidden Planet.* Perf. Walter Pidgeon, Anne Francis, and Leslie Nielsen. 1956.

Chapter 3
Executive Ethics—
The Picture of Dorian Gray

When Dorian Gray entered a room, admiring eyes turned toward him. Sartorially splendid in impeccably tailored bespoke suits of fabulous materials, he exuded effortless class, style and panache. Gentlemen were eager to emulate him, and ladies were anxious to make his acquaintance. As Oscar Wilde described him in his 1890 novel:

> Yes, he was certainly wonderfully handsome, with his finely curved scarlet lips, his frank blue eyes, his crisp gold hair. There was something in his face that made one trust him at once. All the candor of youth was there, as well as youth's passionate purity. One felt that he had kept himself unspotted from the world.

Indeed, it was difficult for people to think ill of him for he projected so powerful an image of decency, culture, innocence and gentility that his true nature was well concealed.

The focus of the novel and the movie is, of course, the wonderful portrait of Dorian painted by the artist Basil Hallward. The artist was enraptured with Dorian and sought to capture his essence, as he perceived it to be, in his greatest work. Hallward's error, though common, was to be deceived by Dorian's natural gifts and attribute to his character and inner being the same perfection that was outwardly obvious. The philosopher Friedrich Nietzsche also noted this classic judgment error:

> Judgments concerning beauty and ugliness are shortsighted but persuasive in the highest degree; they appeal to our instincts where they decide most quickly and pronounce their Yes and No before the understanding can speak.

> ...a whole host of other perfections, originating elsewhere, crystallize around "the particular instance of beauty."

> [Our judgment] lavishes upon the object that inspires it a magic conditioned by the association of various beauty judgments—that are quite alien to the nature of that object. (1887)

Current research lends additional support to Nietzsche's observation that our impressions of a person are almost instantaneous. A team at Princeton found that one-tenth of a second was sufficient for people to infer a specific trait (e.g., good, honest, kind, etc.) when shown an unfamiliar face. Perhaps this is an old race survival tool honed by ten thousand generations of human experience. Now as in the past, our ability to quickly differentiate friend from foe is a vital skill.

The moment the story takes on its enchanted and supernatural aspect occurs when Dorian, gazing upon the finished portrait, makes a heartfelt wish that the painting would age and wither with the passage of the years and he would remain unchanged. Whatever sort of otherworldly entity he invoked remains a mystery, but his prayer was answered. After that moment, neither the debaucheries he indulged in nor the passage of time would mar his countenance.

Teflon Employees:
Dorian in the Workplace

At work we are not necessarily deceived by the influence of good looks alone, but rather by the power of high office and good deeds. Records of achievement, charitable works, community service and other such accomplishments serve to inoculate high corporate officers from suspicion of wrongdoing. Often there is a natural inclination and desire to think well of our leaders. We want to believe we are a part of a good organization led by good people. Unfortunately, our misplaced feelings of confidence and trust are sometimes betrayed when we see past the contrived image and onto the canvas. The CEOs of Enron, WorldCom, Peregrine Financial Group, and BLMIS provide prime examples.

From humble beginnings as the son of a Baptist preacher, Ken Lay's career rose through a series of government and private positions. As CEO and Chairman of Enron from 1985 to 2002, Lay was widely respected and played a prominent role in Texas politics. While at the helm of this giant natural gas supplier and energy-trading firm, Lay received over three dozen honors and awards including: Anti-Defamation League—Torch of Liberty, Houston Community Partners—Father of the Year, Kiwanis Club of Houston— International Executive of the Year, and Rotary Club of Houston— Distinguished Citizen Award.

Mr. Lay was richly compensated, earning up to $42 million per year, and lived accordingly in a $7 million condo while owning 14 other properties. Generous as well, he chartered a boat for $200,000 for his wife's birthday celebration. Were he as generous with the truth, his story might have ended otherwise.

As head of the telecommunications giant, WorldCom, Bernard Ebbers sat atop a conglomerate that was the result of acquiring 60 independent telecom firms in addition to the $40 billion prize of MCI Communications in 1998. The son of a Canadian traveling salesman, Ebbers had come a long way from earning a Bachelor's Degree in Physical Education at Mississippi College and operating a motel chain. Now, he was the subject of honors and accolades including: receiving an honorary Doctor of Laws degree, being inducted into the Mississippi Business Hall of Fame, and being named to The 25 Most Powerful People in Networking by Network World magazine.

Mr. Ebbers was fabulously wealthy with an estimated worth of $1.4 billion including personal holdings such as: a 900-acre ranch in Brookhaven, MS, a yacht and yacht-building firm, 480,000 acres of southern timberland, and a 164,000 acre cattle ranch in British Columbia. Deeply religious, Ebbers regularly taught Sunday School and attended the morning worship service with his family. He reportedly began corporate meetings with a prayer, though apparently some of the Commandments escaped his notice.

Russell Ralph Wasendorf was the namesake of a pastor and his son whose attic provided shelter to the Wasendorfs when money was tight for the Iowa family. The youngest son of a meatpacking plant foreman, he gravitated toward the arts before moving into the futures industry. He founded the Peregrin Financial Group in 1980 using the back room of a barber shop in Cedar Falls for an office. By 2007 Wasendorf was building a $24 million headquarters for PFG and was considered a leading figure in his home town. Always involved in his community, he was on the President's Committee of the University of Iowa and the University of Northern Iowa, contributed gererously to the Cedar Falls Public Library, was a board member of the Greater Cedar Valley Chamber and Alliance, and had pledged $2 million to the UNI athletic program.

He enjoyed an executive lifestyle boasting a $100,000 wine collection, a $7 million jet, a $1 million Chicago condo and a $1 million home outside Cedar Falls. At Chicago's Soldier Field he maintained a luxury suite for Bears' home games, but while looking downfield for another score, this commodity futures quarterback didn't see the sack coming.

No one could have guessed that the son of a plumber born in Queens, NY would grow up to perpetrate the largest financial fraud in U.S. history, but the chairman of BLMIS, otherwise known as Bernard Madoff Financial Services, did just that. Using money earned as a lifeguard and a sprinkler installer combined with a small loan from his father-in-law, he founded BLMIS in 1960.

Madoff and his wife lived the lives of successful financers. His primary residence was a $7 million apartment on Manhattan's Upper East Side, though he also owned an ocean-front residence in Montauk ($3 million), a home in France ($1 million) and a mansion in Palm Beach, Florida ($11 million), where he was a member of the Palm Beach Country Club. Madoff also owned a $7 million 55-foot sportfishing yacht.

Always generous with the money of others, Madoff was a prominent philanthropist. He served as the Chairman of the Board of Directors of the Sy Syms School of Business at Yeshiva University, on the executive council of the Wall Street division of the UJA Foundation of New York, and made philanthropic gifts through the Madoff Family Foundation, a $19 million privately held fund. The foundation made numerous contributions to educational, cultural, and healthcare charities.

Of Things Forbidden by Custom and Law:
The Veil is Lifted

The 1945 movie starred Hurd Hatfield as Dorian but was stolen by George Sanders as Dorian's mentor and chief corrupting influence, Lord Henry. Always the urbane bon vivant, Sanders is perfectly cast and encourages the inquisitive Dorian to explore all the pleasures the world has to offer—no matter where it might take him.

Dorian proves an excellent student and begins visiting less seemly neighborhoods for his entertainment. He becomes smitten with a young, pretty actress in a tawdry theater and attends her performances daily in order to woo her. This ingénue is played by a most delicate Angela Lansbury, who after accepting the aristocratic Dorian into her life is soundly rejected by him and commits suicide. Dorian is unmoved by her death, but his portrait is not. There is now, "…a touch of cruelty in the mouth." as Oscar Wilde wrote. Dorian, at first incredulous, determines that no one can ever again see this reflection of his soul and has the portrait moved to the old schoolroom at the top of the stairs.

In China, the ancient art of face reading called *siang mien* is based upon the belief that a change in our morality or behavior can trigger facial changes—that, aside from the influences of health, time and exposure to the elements, the face we have is the one we've earned. Research on a closely aligned topic at New York University described what Dorian was to next experience. The team found that just as faces may change personality impressions, personality impressions may change the perceptions of faces. More plainly, just as we attribute certain personality traits to an unfamiliar face upon first glance, so may we change our perceptions when provided with additional information.

Dorian's exploits became the subject of vile gossip. Gentlemen of equal station and birth with whom he had often socialized avoided him. Some would leave when he entered a room. Women who had known him on intimate terms were filled with shame in his presence and turned away. Prominent citizens would neither invite him into their homes nor attend his, and friendships with other young men often led to their destruction or disgrace. His youthful purity now seemed a practiced innocence, and perceptions of him changed from refined and ethereal to base and lascivious. The portrait continued to chronicle the putrefaction of his soul.

Concerned with the awful rumors surrounding the subject of his greatest work, Basil Hallward visits Dorian and is received with an uncharacteristic coolness. Basil wants to know if there is any truth to what others are saying, but Dorian fences with him until Basil expresses concern for Dorian's soul. This elicits a sardonic grin from Dorian and he invites the artist to see his soul in the old schoolroom above. Once there, Hallward is aghast at the changes to his work and thinks it a foul joke until he confirms his own signature. Dorian is suddenly seized with a terrible hatred of Hallward as though he were responsible for Dorian's turpitude and murders him in a vicious knife attack.

As with Dorian's reputation, the soaring edifices of integrity and benevolence that girded our corporate CEOs were eventually seen as shallow façades—thin veneers of decency that cloaked rapacious spirits.

Ken Lay's **Enron** collapsed in late 2001. For years financial reports had exaggerated assets and minimized or failed to report loses and liabilities. Investors saw $70 billion evaporate. Trustees and employees lost $2 billion in pension funds, stock options and savings plans. To sully his own soul's portrait even further, as Lay dumped large amounts of his Enron stock in September and October 2001, he encouraged his employees to buy more stock, telling them the company would rebound. Lay liquidated more than $300 million of Enron stock from 1998 to 2001. In the end, the stock that sold for $90 per share was worth 60 cents.

The tale of one retiree helps put a human face on this disaster. George Maddox was a plant manager for 30 years with the company. All his retirement savings were invested in 14,000 shares of Enron stock, formerly worth more than $1.3 million. When the stock became worthless, Maddox, now 78, and his wife Phyllis had to go back to work. Phyllis, a retired teacher, began serving as a substitute while George mowed lawns and pastures. They also had to lease their suburban Houston home and move into an old family farmhouse. Phyllis later developed liver cancer and died in 2008. George is raising his grandson by himself.

WorldCom collapsed in 2003 with Bernard Ebbers at the helm. The $11 billion fraud was based upon phony earnings reports and caused a $60 dollar stock to become a penny stock. Billions in shareholder value were destroyed, and as with Enron, the retirement savings of thousands vanished. WorldCom used shady accounting methods to mask its declining financial condition by falsely reporting financial growth and profitability to increase the price of WorldCom's stock.

The damage wasn't limited to WorldCom and its employees, though. AT&T fired tens of thousands in the late 1990s as it tried to compete with WorldCom's falsely claimed low costs. Those employees did not need to be fired, but it was too late for them once the fraud was revealed.

Peregrine Financial Group met its end in July 2012. Russell R. Wasendorf had been stealing customer funds for twenty years and had forged confidential documents that the National Futures Association (NFA) uses to verify cash deposits held by a broker. Apparently, Wasendorf intercepted letters being sent by the NFA to U.S. Bank, where Peregrine had its major deposits, and forged signatures and wildly inflated bank balances on the documents that he then mailed back to the regulatory organization. Wasendorf had set up a post office box in Cedar Falls, Iowa and it was to that box that the NFA sent the documents, which were addressed to the bank. The post office box was neither in Wasendorf's name nor registered to the bank.

While small in scale compared to the other cases, over $215 million in investor's funds are missing. In order to ensure his portrait's further decay, hundreds of SpongeBob SquarePants silver coins, thought to be in the possession of Wasendorf, cannot be located. The coins of the popular TV cartoon character were manufactured as novelty items for customer purchase.

Bernard Madoff stated he began his Ponzi scheme at **BLMIS** in 1991. After its collapse in 2008 he admitted he had never made any legitimate investments with his clients' money during that entire time. Instead, he simply deposited the money into his personal business account at Chase Manhattan Bank. When his customers asked for withdrawals, he paid them out of the Chase account, effectively paying one investor with the money of another.

Not only were personal investments destroyed and retirements ruined, but affected institutions included charitable foundations such as the one Elie Wiesel established to foster international dialogue, (entire funding of $15.2 million lost), and Steven Spielberg's Wunderkinder Foundation that entrusted Madoff with 70 percent of its dividend and interest income in 2006. Philanthropic federations and hospitals lost millions of dollars, forcing some organizations to close. The Lappin Foundation, for example, was forced to temporarily close because it had placed its entire $8 million endowment in his hands..

Dorian at Work:
Managing and Recruiting Do's and Don'ts

DO:
- Establish company-wide integrity principles the leaders are held accountable for enforcing.
- Include integrity questions in annual survey.
- Conduct 360° assessments of CEO and top leadership to explore integrity questions.
- Communicate that integrity must not be compromised to make the numbers.
- Discuss integrity issues at staff meetings.
- Protect "whistle blowers."
- Establish integrity specifications for successor selection.

- Ask how candidates have handled ethical issues in the past.
- Use multiple interviewers who will verify information.
- Check resume for serious deletions of critical information or those that include misleading information.
- Conduct thorough background checks.

DON'T

- Fail to discipline top of organization as well as bottom for violations of integrity code.
- Place low status individuals in charge of infrastructure for enforcing integrity culture; put the "A" Team in.
- Delay response to early warning signals.
- Ignore concerns or superficially investigate.
- Avoid asking hard questions to high-level candidates out of concern for their feelings.
- Start taking notes immediately if candidates admit to ethical lapses. They might stop talking. Wait until later to record responses.
- Take notes that judge the candidate. Just describe what is seen and heard.
- Ask theoretical questions that require speculation. Ask behavioral questions that require specific examples from experience.

Retribution:
A Painful Reckoning

After the murder and disposal of the artist Hallward, Dorian attempts to resume his decadent ways but is hampered by a resurgent conscience. The portrait, which he furtively slips in to see from time to time, is now a hellhound of seething blood-drenched corruption staring back at him. Its image haunts his dreams and gives him no rest.

Dorian concludes that if evil deeds spoiled the portrait, good deeds will restore it. In a supposed grand gesture of self-denial, he breaks off a rendez-vous with a sweet country girl named Hetty Merton, thereby leaving her and her honor intact. He then rushes back to view his portrait hoping to find some improvement in it. He is dismayed when he finds none and, in fact, sees the decay continuing. Enraged at the object of his torment, he lunges at it with the same knife he used on Hallward. The night air is torn with a piercing scream.

After some minutes the servants gather enough courage to enter the old schoolroom. Peering cautiously, they first see the portrait as they remembered it with their master in his splendid youth. Lying on the floor was a dead man whose features were so withered and distorted that it was not until they examined his rings that they realized who it was. Dorian left this world with the face he had earned.

The final curtain doesn't descend upon our corporate Dorians with the same melodramatic flourish. The details and complexities of each case were painstakingly ground through the legal system until the judgments emerged.

Ken Lay was convicted on all six counts against him including conspiracy to commit securities fraud and wire fraud while leading Enron. He faced a maximum of 45 years in jail with an additional 120 years in a separate case. While out on bail awaiting sentencing however, Lay, 64, suffered a fatal heart attack at his Colorado retreat and died without having served a single day.

Bernard Ebbers, 65, was found guilty of all counts against him including conspiracy, securities fraud and false regulatory filings. He was sentenced to twenty-five years in prison at the Oakdale, Louisiana Federal Correctional Institution.

Peregrine's Wasendorf pleaded guilty to charges including mail fraud, embezzling customer funds and making false statements to two regulatory agencies. He was sentenced to 50 years in prison and ordered to pay $215.5 million in restitution. Prior to his confession, Wasendorf, 64, attempted suicide.

On March 12, 2009, Bernard Madoff, 71, pled guilty to 11 federal felonies, including securities fraud, wire fraud, mail fraud, money laundering, making false statements, perjury, theft from an employee benefit plan, and making false filings with the SEC. He was sentenced to 150 years imprisonment and forfeiture of $17 billion. He is currently inmate #6661727-054 at the Butner Federal Correctional Complex in North Carolina with a release date of 11-14-2139.

His eldest son, Mark, committed suicide on the second anniversary of the crime's reporting.

What is clear from all these cases is the huge cost paid by firms for allowing dishonesty to prevail. Aside from the obvious legal difficulties, a host of other problems may ensue. A firm's reputation may be damaged beyond repair, and opportunities for new and repeat business strongly diminished. Current employees can become uncomfortable with such a culture and demonstrate their unhappiness through increased absenteeism and turnover, while recruiting key replacements may prove impossible. Additionally, certain controls can reach insufferable levels if firms resort to employee surveillance through electronic monitoring, and closer government scrutiny can take its toll as well.

Dorian Gray unfolds as a classic morality play, though at its publication was considered sinful and scandalous by the literary press. It proves the adage regarding the wages of sin, yet never describes them fully. As Oscar Wilde remarked when interviewed by the *Scots Observer* upon the debut of his novel, "Each man sees his own sin in Dorian Gray. What Dorian Gray's sins are no one knows. He who finds them has brought them." (July 12, 1890)

As did Dorian, these CEOs each had a portrait, hung perhaps in a closed off room called conscience. Did they dare peek, when the night was still, to see how it fared?

References

Birchfield, Reg. "Honesty at the Top." *New Zealand Management*. Mar 2004: 70-1.

Bunge, et al. "Peregrine." *Wall Street Journal* [New York] 18 Jul 2012, Web.

Byham, William C. "Can You Interview for Integrity." *Across the Board*. Mar 2004: 35-8.

Chew, Robert. "Madoff's Victims: Finding Meaning in the Devastation." *Time*. 30 Dec 2008: n. page. Web.

Cialdini, Robert B. et al. "The Hidden Costs of Organizational Dishonesty." *Sloan Management Review*. Spr 2004: 67-73.

Hassin, Ran, and Yaacov Trope. "Facing Faces: Studies on the Cognitive Aspects of Physiognomy." *Journal of Personality and Social Psychology*. 78.5 (2000): 837-52.

Heineman, Ben W. "The Fatal Flaw in Pay for Performance." *Harvard Business Review*. Jun 2008: 31-34.

Lavelle, Marianne, et al. "Rogues of the Year." *U.S. News & World Report*. 30 Dec 2002: 32-42.

Lewin, Albert, dir. *The Picture of Dorian Gray*. Perf. George Sanders. 1945. Film.

McClam, "WorldCom victims focusing on trial." *Deseret News* 14 Jan 2005, Web.

Neitzsche, Friedrich. Trans. *The Will To Power*. Walter Kaufmann. New York: Vintage Books, 1968. 423-25.

The Associated Press, "Enron's victims: still angry, but coping." *Omaha World-Herald* 3 Dec 2011, Web.

Wilde, Oscar. *The Picture of Dorian Gray*. New York: Barnes & Noble Books, 2003.

Willis, Janine, and Alexander Todorov. "First Impressions." *Psychological Science*. 17.7 (2006): 592-98.

WALTER WANGER CREATES THE ULTIMATE IN SCIENCE-FICTION!
INVASION OF THE
BODY SNATCHERS
COLLIER'S MAGAZINE
called it
"THE NIGHTMARE THAT
THREATENS THE WORLD"
AN
ALLIED ARTISTS
PICTURE
starring
KEVIN McCARTHY · DANA WYNTER
with LARRY GATES · KING DONOVAN · CAROLYN JONES · JEAN WILLES · RALPH DUMKE
Directed by DON SIEGEL · Screenplay by DANIEL MAINWARING · Based on the COLLIER'S MAGAZINE Serial by JACK FINNEY
FILMED IN
SUPERSCOPE

Chapter 4
Controlling Consultants—
Invasion of the Body
Snatchers

Santa Mira, California was the archetype of small town America. A close-knit, middle class community of people living well ordered lives, raising families, sure of themselves and their neighbors, comfortable in the world. There was one problem, though—a growing sense of alienation from friends and relatives was gripping the townsfolk.

Almost indefinably, old friends no longer knew each other, children felt estranged from their parents, and a palpable sense of unease was viral in its spread. So begins the 1956 thriller *Invasion of the Body Snatchers*, starring Kevin McCarthy as Dr. Miles Bennell and Dana Wynter as his fiancée Becky Driscoll. The movie plays upon some of our most intimate fears—that those closest to us are really replacements, proxies, doubles, or changelings—whose outward appearance is normal and reassuring, but whose mind and spirit are completely foreign.

The allure of the invaders, (in this case extraterrestrial seed pods that replicate the victims' bodies and steal their minds when they fall asleep) is the promise of a life devoid of emotion—no joy, no fear. All is replaced with an overwhelming calm and an unconcerned confidence in the future. Sound familiar? Perhaps you've just signed an agreement with a management consultant!

How well founded though, is this sense of confidence? While imported experts can make significant contributions to a business, their counsel can also lead to neutral or even negative results. For example, between 1989 and 1994 AT&T was billed over $500 million for consulting services provided by firms such as McKinsey & Co., and emerged no better than before.

Sears engaged Harvard professor Michael Porter's Monitor firm in the late 1980s and adopted the disastrous "every day low pricing" scheme. Though this strategy resulted in Sears making dramatic, permanent price cuts on a wide variety of items, it ran counter to what their customers expected—periodic, deep-discount sales. It additionally placed them in direct competition with low-cost operations like Wal-Mart. Sears received this counsel at no discount to itself. The company had 40 to 50 Monitor consultants present during this time, each charging $2,000 to $2,500 per day.

Conversely, when Sears engaged A.T. Kearney in 1993, the recommendation to change sourcing for their DieHard battery reduced costs by 20%. There are numerous other examples, but what's clear is that the results are mixed. Hiring a consultant does not guarantee success. Why then their popularity?

Rational vs. Emotional:
"Once you understand, you'll be grateful."

Good reasons abound for employing one. The growth in government bureaucracies has forced business to comply with an avalanche of new regulations, from the EPA to Sarbanes-Oxley. Bringing in a consultant to guide a firm through the wilderness and in some cases perform the audits themselves makes sense. Likewise, the need for specialized expertise, talent, skills or temporary technical assistance, e.g., installing a new IT system, is highly justifiable. If a training staff is overburdened or nonexistent, it is common practice to have consultants instruct as required. Additionally, if a valued employee is in dire need of personal coaching to either advance or save their career, another good use for consultants is apparent.

However, the confluence of four key factors can lead firms to lower their defenses and enable the invasion:

1. The availability of funds.
2. A high-pressure organization seeking leading-edge innovations.
3. An insecure manager promoted beyond his self-perceived level of competence.
4. A slick consulting firm cleverly marketing management fads.

Simply put, if money is budgeted and the business is seeking rapid improvement or growth, an insecure or overly ambitious manager can be an easy mark for consultants selling a wholesale organizational transformation.

The Sale:
"Now relax, we're here to help you."

Were those words spoken by a consultant to an uncertain client? No, but they *were* spoken by neighbor and friend Jack Belicec to Miles and Becky in an attempt to convince them to surrender to the alien seduction as he already had.

Consulting firms inspire confidence in their potential clients—cause them to relax—by sending in their senior partners first. These sartorially splendid ambassadors exude competence, rank and savvy. They are most of all, however, pitchmen hawking their firm's wares, as a street peddler would sell ties out of a suitcase. What they don't reveal though, is their intention of becoming disengaged project managers supervising teams of Associate Consultants, (a.k.a. apprentices with MBAs) who will learn their trade at your expense.

Oftentimes the senior partner will drop the names of famous firms who have used their services to *transform* their businesses, followed by the threat of a dismal future for firms that do not. Once the hiring executive is properly hooked on this narrative, a systematic program for implementation is suggested, whether it be for TQM, JIT, MBO, MRP, Re-engineering or any of the hundreds of other possibilities.

Shortly thereafter the senior partner will produce a formal proposal, (written on the finest stationery and packaged in a presentation-grade folder) that makes vague and grand promises with equally vague deliverables devoid of milestones:

The outstanding team of engineering consultants from Dynamic Bombast LLC, with its reputation for world-class service, will provide innovative and flexible solutions to ensure that Lock, Stock and Barrel Corporation receives unparalleled comprehensive technical support as it endeavors to achieve ever higher levels of excellence.

Sign here_____x.

Working with Consultants:
"They'll absorb your minds, your memories. You'll be reborn into an untroubled world!"

After much planning and confidential discussions with the hiring executive, a kickoff meeting is held where all the top managers are brought together. More than a casual introduction, it turns into a pep rally designed to build momentum and generate high spirits. Commitment is sought, even demanded by the consultant—all under the benevolent gaze of the executive. The wise get onboard.

The consultant looks for supporters, potential converts, and most especially, skeptics, cynics and adversaries. The latter have to be identified early on and either converted, isolated, neutralized or removed. Shortly, the consultant will share those concerns with the executive.

Training (a.k.a. indoctrination) begins for the staff and they are introduced to consultant-speak. The new vocabulary, that they will be requested to use at all times, will include such words and phrases as: B2B, bandwidth, drill down, buckets, buttoned-up, deliverables, fact pack, granular, takeaway, value-stream, etc.

Those most adept at mastering this Newspeak will be identified as high-potential individuals. Their futures will soon be linked to the success of the project.

The infiltration continues now at an accelerated pace. All formality is dispensed with and the consultant named Mr. Smith becomes "Chuck." Chuck will take key staffers out to lunch regularly and ply them for intimate details about their firm, their co-workers, their boss, and their concerns. He will use this information to make recommendations to the executive that will astound with their perceptiveness and insight.

This honeymoon phase will last from weeks to months and be characterized by high emotional commitment, uncritical euphoria, rampant use of the new vocabulary, and most importantly—seeding. The high-potential individuals earlier identified will be placed on "special assignment" and provided in-depth schooling by the consulting firm. When they return from their initiation they will be seeded (remember the pods) throughout the organization to instruct and to guide the progress of departmental-level initiatives. They will also act as spies for the consultant and executive. Woe be unto the employee who does not demonstrate mindless enthusiasm!

The Honeymoon is Over:
"I've got to stop them!"

The blush is off the rose. Managers and their staffs have worked tirelessly with the consultants. They have answered questions, provided data and orientations, attended endless meetings, watched and given presentations, used the Newspeak words, been affable and cooperative—and it is never enough. The consultants are getting underfoot.

The managers have noticed that the consultants have easier access to the executive than they do. They notice that a consultant is providing an annoying presence in formerly staff-only meetings. They've begun to consider the consultants as parasitic and they suspect their confidentiality. Their lack of specific industry knowledge is infuriating and some suspect that they're being presented with repackaged ideas—old wine in new bottles.

The staff views the executive in a dimmer light. He is seen as less competent each time he reaches out to the consultant for advice, counsel, or even confidence. One of them remarks that just as Dumbo the elephant (in the classic Disney cartoon), needed to clutch the "magic" feather in order to believe he could fly, so the boss clings to the consultant.

Some feel the consultants are arrogant and pushy. Others see the consultants as threats to their expertise, identities, careers, and even jobs. The managers slowly withdraw their cooperation. They become less available, harder to find, evasive, less forthcoming and generally taciturn. If they are risk takers they will attempt to inform the executive of their concerns and doubts. If they are risk averse they will remain silent and exert minimum effort.

Soon it becomes obvious that something is wrong. The results are not there. The deliverables are not being delivered. Things are not buttoned-up and the company had better drill down to find out why this expensive undertaking is not producing the desired results. What to do!

How to Manage a Consultant:
"Then, out of the sky, came a solution…"

Consultancies are generally resistant to evaluation or systematic monitoring, but that is exactly what must be done. They must be held accountable as any employee is regardless of rank. Establishing accountability should occur at the outset, when sales pitches are glistening and negotiations just starting.

The company defines the scope of the engagement, not the consultant. A company must never prostrate itself in front of a consulting firm and defer to its superior wisdom and experience. The company knows its business and its industry. If it is uncertain as to the exact nature of the problem it is experiencing, it should tightly prescribe the diagnostic intervention. The consultant may want to go fishing with a net. Give him a spear.

Consultants may provide tremendous value if successful and should be supplied with a supportive environment. The physical workplace furnished should be conducive to the type of work to be done. Placing them in a closet with a single light bulb hanging from the ceiling won't work! Support personnel should be assigned as required. No firm should be paying a consultant to stand at a copier.

Communications should flow freely in both directions, and if the consultant is going astray, provide rapid feedback so that a course change won't entail a long excursion toward a wrong heading. Assign a staff member as a focal point for the consultant so that orientations, introductions and appointments are crisply accomplished. A consultant should never be wandering the halls trying to locate a person or a room.

The written contract is all-important. It must contain clear objectives and delineate specific milestones that scheduled progress reports will document. A failure to reach targets on schedule must trigger increased scrutiny from the highest levels. One way to encourage consultants to be timely in their work is by linking fee payments to the completion of an important phase of the work.

If the consultancy is sending a team to your business, insist on knowing the capabilities of each member. Get their business biographies so the suitability of the individuals to the task is apparent. Accordingly, the finest people from the client firm must be provided to the consultants if requested. The best possible results will ensue, and any training they receive will add to their personal development and value to the firm.

Consultants typically attempt to ingratiate themselves to the client firm in the hopes of gaining follow-on assignments. However, the wise executive, regardless of comfort level with the current firm, will not use them if the skills are not appropriate for the next task.

James O. McKinsey, the revered founder of his namesake firm and the management consulting industry, was CEO of Marshall Field & Co., (the great Chicago department store retailer) in 1937. He had a troubled time there and was on the verge of being fired when he contracted pneumonia and died at the age of 47. The day before he died he told a former friend and client that making real decisions in a business is a lot tougher than providing advice.

This is what must be kept in mind when working with consultants. They have skills and know a craft, but the employees know their company and must always keep that knowledge near when being advised about what's right for the firm. So don't fall asleep when working with consultants. You don't want your body, or your wallet, snatched!

References

Gill, John, and Sue Whittle. "Management By Panacea: Accounting For Transience." *Journal of Management Studies*. 30.2 (1992): 281-95.

O'Shea, James, and Charles Madigan. *Dangerous Company*. New York: Random House, 1997.

Perchthold, Gordon, and Jenny Sutton. *Extract Value From Consultants*. 1st ed. Austin, TX: Greenleaf Book Group Press, 2010.

Russ, Banham. "Have No Fear, The Consultants Are Here." *CFO Magazine*. Jun 2010: 56-9.

Shenson, Howard. *How to Select and Manage Consultants*. Lexington, MA: Lexington Books, 1990.

Siegel, Don, dir. *Invasion of the Body Snatchers*. Perf. Kevin McCarthy, and Dana Wynter. 1955. Film.

Sturdy, Andrew. "The Consultancy Process - An Insecure Business?." *Journal of Management Studies*. 34.3 (1997): 389-413.

Chapter 5
Succession Planning—
Tower of London

A beheading axe in 15th century England had a handle two feet long attached to a heavy, curved blade. A pike of similar vintage was from nine to twelve feet long and consisted of a wooden pole with a narrow, pointed blade at the end. The former was used to sever the head, the latter to display it. If one were fortunate, a single blow would suffice.

In times long past, battles for the throne of England were bloody affairs, and the 1939 classic *Tower of London* tells the tale of one of the most vicious and disruptive episodes in British royal history. The genesis was the incredibly complex series of multi-generational arranged marriages, between descendants of a king, that resulted in such confusion that a rightful heir could not be agreed upon. The stakes being vast wealth, land holdings, castles, huge estates, titles of nobility and political power, the contesting families were willing to resort to any and all means to achieve their goals. The chaos and mayhem created by the Wars of the Roses is the ultimate expression of succession planning gone awry.

The King was Edward III, and of his seven sons, two great branches of the family, the houses of Lancaster and York (whose symbols were the red and white rose respectively) were founded by John of Gaunt, Duke of Lancaster and Edmund, Duke of York. This drama revolves around one grandson of Edmund, namely Richard, Duke of Gloucester, later to become Richard III.

Preparing to Lead:
Heirs Apparent for the Throne Room or Board Room

While the necessary developmental activities and desired qualities for medieval kings and current CEOs form a happy confluence, one trusts the use of deportations, abductions, denouncements and assassinations has lost its frequency of use in the modern corporation. Will it be the pen or the pike?

Tales of Richard's distorted appearance have endured for centuries, but history has only recently provided reliable corroboration with the discovery of what is thought to be his burial site. The skeleton reveals a curved spine that lends support to tales describing him as a hunchback. He was said to have been born with long hair and a full set of teeth, but most likely his deeds led his enemies to encourage such descriptions. Portraits show a trim body and a delicate face.

Richard was eight when his father, Prince Richard of York, was killed in battle with the Lancasters. He had two older brothers, Edward and George. Edward, the eldest and ten years his senior, became King Edward IV by decree from the great barons, nobles and officers of state. At the age of nineteen Richard was made Duke of Gloucester and his middle brother George, Duke of Clarence.

Nobles of high rank like Richard and his brothers were fitted at an early age with suits of armor. These were quite expensive, and when worn in their entirety, quite heavy. To develop a martial bearing and the skills needed for armed combat, strenuous training was applied. They were challenged, while wearing armor, to run races, mount a horse by leaping from the ground, deliver a fusillade of blows with axe, sword or club, climb ladders with only the use of hands, and play the quintaine.

The quintaine was a device designed to sharpen the skills of a mounted knight at full tilt. It consisted of a ten to twelve foot post anchored in the ground across the top of which a pivoting crossbar was attached. Hanging from the ends of the crossbar were two objects—a target and a club. The competitors were to ride at full gallop toward the quintaine and deliver a powerful strike with either a hurled spear or a lance that would cause the crossbar to rotate swiftly on its axis and threaten the rider with a sharp blow to the head from the club if he were insufficiently evasive. The idea was to simulate a crowded battlefield in which one might be engaging an enemy to the front, while being threatened by an enemy behind. In all these matters brother George was far more athletic than Richard, (though Basil Rathbone's portrayal of Richard in the film includes very skillful sparring sessions with halberds and short and long swords).

From 1471 to 1483 Richard established himself as the dominant noble in the north of England. The stability he brought to the region through his leadership skills was rare for that time and much appreciated. He acquired numerous titles of merit including Warden of the West March, Keeper of the Forests, Sheriff of Cumberland, and was able to unite the interests of powerful earls in the North Country.

Grooming a modern, high-potential manager for executive service has its own typically rigorous schedule, as it is widely recognized that the move from functional to general management is a large leap. After performing well as an individual contributor, the classic progression sequence is:

- Managing—
  - Others
  - Other managers
  - Entire functions (Marketing, Engineering, etc.)
  - Businesses (An entire division or product line as a profit center)
  - Other General Managers
  - Enterprise

Michael Eisner, Chairman and CEO of Walt Disney Productions from 1984 to 2005, traced that classic arc. After graduating from college in 1964, Eisner became a clerk at NBC and left there after six weeks to join CBS in their programming department. Dissatisfied with the challenges and opportunities there, he mailed out numerous resumes and was hired by ABC where he was promoted to a production executive in children's programming. By 1968 he was named director of program development for the East Coast.

Enjoying great success in the 1970s, Eisner rose to Senior VP of primetime production and development for ABC Entertainment. In 1976 he left television to become president and COO of Paramount Pictures under his mentor, Barry Diller. Eisner left Paramount in 1984 to become Chairman and CEO of The Walt Disney Company. When he arrived at Disney, nearly 80% of the revenues, totaling about $1.7 billion, were from theme parks. Ten years later, with revenues over $10 billion, almost $5 billion came from Disney films, $3.5 billion came from the parks, and almost $2 billion from Disney merchandise.

In 2005, amid challenges from stockholders and Disney family members calling for new leadership, Eisner stepped down. *Conversations With Michael Eisner*, an entertainment/interview program on the CNBC television network followed thereafter, and was filmed at the same New York studio where Eisner worked as a page in the 1960s.

The Eisner-type career was the model twenty or more years ago. Now, however, a new model has taken hold that values broad experience over narrow, and international assignments are key. Fully three-quarters of Fortune 100 CEOs today have spent at least two years working overseas in senior positions. Decades ago such a move would often take a promising executive off the career track to the corner office and relegate him to expatriate limbo. Now, with interwoven global alliances more the norm than exception, knowledge of managing complex relationships among diverse cultures is extremely valuable. The career path of Sergio Marchionne, CEO of Fiat, Chairman and CEO of Chrysler Group LLC, and Chairman of Fiat Industrial, describes the new archetype.

Born in Abruzzo, Italy of Italian and Croatian parents, Marchionne immigrated with his family to Toronto, Canada at age fourteen. After finishing his schooling in 1983 with an MBA and a law degree, he worked initially as a tax and accounting specialist for Deloitte & Touche before launching upon a mercurial career trajectory. His industrial exposure includes firms working in gas exploration, commercial packaging, industrial supply, aluminum production, and precision inspection, verification and testing.

Never one to let the moss grow beneath him, he filled financial and legal executive roles for five different companies within eleven years. His career took him to Zurich, Switzerland in 1994 with the Alusuisse Lonza smelting firm where he was made CEO three years later. After part of that business was spun off, he moved to Basel, Switzerland to serve as CEO and Chairman till 2002. He then moved to Geneva in February of that year to become CEO of SGS S.A., a Swiss precision measurement and quality assurance firm.

Most importantly, while at SGS Marchionne was elected as an independent member of the Board of Directors of Fiat S.p.A. and appointed CEO in 2004. When Chrysler emerged from Chapter 11 bankruptcy protection in 2009, Fiat received a 20% stake in the Chrysler Group and he was appointed CEO. Three years later he was made Chairman when Fiat increased its stake to 53.5%. A capable executive with multi-industry, multi-national experience can write his own succession plan.

Qualities of a King or CEO:
Leadership, Coalition Building, Politics

What are the qualities to be sought in a king? As any individual presiding over a complex organization, a king has multiple roles and responsibilities. A king must be able to:

- Build and maintain key alliances
  - With the landed gentry (who ranked just below the nobles)
  - With the nobility—powerful families with great wealth and private armies must be kept in close alignment, hence the importance of arranged marriages and bloodlines.

- Enlist the support of traditional institutions
  - Parliament
  - The Church
  - The people

- Defend the realm
  - Maintain the loyalty of key generals and the fighting forces
  - Supply and maintain those forces

- Conduct foreign relations
  - Negotiate treaties and regulate commerce with neighboring countries, notably France and Spain
  - Arrange marriages as a function of strategy

- Control the budget
  - Manage the treasury
  - See to the effective utilization of estate lands
  - Raise funds through rents, sales, taxation

Beyond the tasks there is the matter of royal deportment. How one displays one's character, or how one conceals it, is an essential part of statecraft. Machiavelli's sage advice offered in *The Prince* (1532) is still current and fresh:

> ...Thus it is well to seem merciful, faithful, humane, sincere, religious, and also to be so; but you must have the mind so disposed that when it is needful to be otherwise you may be able to change to the opposite qualities. And it must be understood that a prince, and especially a new prince, cannot observe all those things which are considered good in men, being often obliged, in order to maintain the state, to act against faith, against charity, against humanity, and against religion.

Richard had proved himself an able leader and had a loyal following among the higher gentry in the north. He was also head of the Council of the North, and was responsible for the financial, judicial and administrative operations of a huge region. His reputation held that he was evenhanded and knowledgeable.

He rewarded fidelity with fidelity to such an extent that he would, perhaps unwisely, support the gentry over the nobles in contests for land or influence.

His brother, Edward IV, had to intervene to prevent Richard from challenging Lord Thomas Stanley's power in the northwest. Richard's instincts to feel indebtedness toward lower ranked men who had fought beside him in past battles rather than accede to the wishes of the nobility was admirable, but would prove costly.

As for the CEO, what qualities are to be sought? Multiple roles and responsibilities are features of the modern CEO's job as well. An effective CEO must be able to:

- Build and maintain key alliances
    - With the Board of Directors, major executives and staff
    - With large stockholders, institutional investors, investment funds
    - With stock analysts and ratings firms

- Enlist the support of traditional institutions
    - Government: local, state, federal and functionaries—EPA, OSHA, etc.
    - Banks
    - Public: Assorted non-profit organizations, good neighbor policies

- Defend the realm
    - Environmental scanning to detect competitive threats
    - New product and service development to promote growth
    - Attract and retain key talent

- Conduct foreign relations
    - Manage key customers, suppliers and trade partners
    - Manage co-production and subcontracting relations
    - Merge and acquire

- Control the budget
    - Maintain spending and investment to support strategy
    - Act as steward of corporate resources
    - Support regulation and reporting requirements, e.g., IRS, SOX

Moreover, in the search for a new CEO, the Board of Directors must agree on the desired qualities of that person. Does the firm need the same type of person as the one departing or someone quite different? If the company began as a start-up with an entrepreneur at the helm, is it now in need of an expert administrator to manage growth and coordinate complex systems, or does it need more of the same? The Board's agreement is critical to a successful search.

Proctor & Gamble uses this eleven point criteria for its senior executives:

- Character, values, and integrity
- Proven track record: business, financial, and organization performance
- Capability and capacity builder
- High energy and high endurance
- Visionary and strategic leader
- Inspiring, courageous, and compassionate
- Productive relationships with colleagues, partners, and other external stakeholders
- Embraces change. Leads transformational change
- Calm, cool, and resilient in the face of conflict and criticism
- Institution builder
- Prioritizes greater good and longer-term health of the company

The list well incorporates the performance-oriented criteria established by classic scholars of organizational management, e.g., Fayol, Gulick, Mooney and Reiley, etc., who espoused task-oriented competencies (i.e., planning, organizing, coordinating and controlling) with more humanistic qualities stressing the importance of promoting cooperative systems by demonstrating leadership and character.

Failing to build and maintain key alliances with the board, major executives and staff remains a primary reason for early CEO departure. For example, while Robert E. Allen was CEO of AT&T he actively ran the search for his own replacement, finally selecting John Walter as his understudy in the COO position. After seven months, the board decided not to promote him to the top spot. Buying out his contract cost the company $26 million.

In another instance, John P. Reilly served as president of Brunswick for nine months until a clash with VP Dianne Yaconetti led to his ouster prior to promotion. In both cases relationships, not performance, determined the outcome. Over 30% of heirs apparent do not make it to CEO, but only 10-15% of CEOs are dismissed by their boards. It is easier to stop a prince's ascension than to dethrone a king.

Ascending to the Throne or Corner Office:
Obstacles and Opponents

Richard was the twelfth of Cecily Neville's thirteen children and the youngest of seven who survived infancy. His older brother, Edward IV ruled England after defeating Lancastrian forces at the Battle of Tewksbury in 1471.

Richard had his own designs on the throne, but according to the laws of succession, had several obstacles in his path. Aside from his eldest brother Edward, there was his brother George, Duke of Clarence, his senior by three years, and most importantly the two young sons of Edward. As fate would have it, George removed himself from Richard's way in a very bloody episode.

The relationship between Edward and George was never close, and deteriorated sharply after Edward returned from a military expedition in France with huge amounts of debt. To secure the needed funds Edward caused Parliament to pass a law that placed all the inheritances from his father, which had been divided into thirds and shared among the three brothers, at the service of the crown.

George was outraged at this and expressed his anger openly. He retreated from London with his wife Isabella to a castle far into the countryside, and sulked. Some months later she gave birth to their second son, but unfortunately never regained her strength and died a few months later.

During this period belief in witchcraft and sorcery was strong. George was convinced his wife's death was due to either supernatural forces or poisoning, and believed the queen, Edward's wife, was behind it all. He identified a woman he thought had been employed by the queen for this purpose and sent armed men to bring her back to Warwick castle. Within three hours of entering Warwick she was tried, condemned and executed. Edward and the queen heard of this and were furious at the accusation.

Shortly afterwards, a nobleman friend of the king died. Edward accused a priest of killing him by use of sorcery. The priest was arrested and tortured to gain a confession and the names of any accomplices. He confessed under torture and also offered the name of a man who was a member of George's household and a trusted confidant. Both men were immediately executed.

At the news of this George exploded, traveled to London and stormed into the king's council chamber and denounced the king and all who support him as unjust, cruel tyrants. Edward was not present at this outburst, but word quickly reached him and George was arrested for subversion and taken to the Tower. George was brought to trial before the House of Lords where he was accused of treason, conspiracy to depose the king, joining forces with the Lancasters, and having a secret armed force waiting to strike. He was condemned to death and taken back to the Tower.

Considering a public execution of his own brother to be rather bad form, assassins were enlisted, allegedly with the aid of Richard, to visit George's chambers in the Tower and kill him. In the movie, Boris Karloff plays a worshipful, club-footed henchman to Richard named Mord, who after witnessing a drinking contest between the two brothers drowns George, Duke of Clarence, in a huge vat of Malmsey, a much favored sweet, white fortified wine.

King Edward IV was next to depart, this time of natural causes, albeit accelerated by personal indulgences. After the death of brother George in 1478, Edward adopted a life of debauchery so weakening his natural forces that he finally succumbed to his dissipated state six years later at the age of forty-one. That left Edward's two young sons, Edward V and Richard of Shrewsbury, next in line to the throne. Richard (III), Duke of Gloucester did not want Edward crowned.

A high council in London decided that instead of Richard (III) ruling, a ruling council would be established with Richard at its head. He demanded that he be made Protector of Edward's children as was his right and Edward's will. This was accepted and as Edward V's party was approaching London from the south, Richard seized the twelve-year-old child, sent him to the Tower, and had several members of his escort executed without trial on charges of treason. The child's younger brother and mother requested and were granted sanctuary in the Church, though it was later revoked by the Archbishop of Canterbury under Richard's influence. This led to both brothers being held together in the Tower.

Richard then sought to have Edward's two sons declared illegitimate on the grounds that Edward IV had been previously contracted to marry another. Parliament agreed, in part due to Richard's terrifying countenance, and offered him the throne June 26, 1483. His coronation took place at Westminster Abbey in July, and after that following September the two young princes were never seen again.

King Richard suspected rebellion was brewing in the south, and as many new CEOs, supplanted the regional officers there with his own trusted men from the north. Edward IV had strong support in London and the south, as well as from the Church and papal legation. Richard's support was in the less populated north, and the Church was divided in its view of him. Powerful forces were aligning themselves against Richard, as in the minds of many his coronation settled nothing.

Succession events in a closely held family business are no less fraught with emotion. Relationships with siblings are set early and memories endure. Birth rank matters, as does the sting of favoritism. The resultant hard feelings and jealously can linger for decades and erupt when the day of reckoning for issues of ownership and control arrives.

Smooth transfers of responsibility can and do occur as evidenced by:

- James Dolan succeeding his father Charles at Cablevision Systems
- Donald Graham succeeding his mother Katherine at The Washington Post
- Christie Hefner succeeding her father Hugh at Playboy

Yet lineage is not always sufficient to guarantee happy transitions.

- Abigail Johnson was derailed by her father Ned of Fidelity Investments
- Shari Redstone was undervalued by her father Sumner of Viacom
- Lachlan Murdoch left News Corporation over an inheritance dispute with Rupert

Murder and betrayal though, are not just reserved for royalty. The iconic U-Haul corporation was founded in 1945 by Leonard S. Shoen at the age of twenty-nine with a loan of $5,000 from family friends. His hunch that returning military personnel would be relocating all across the country was correct, and the result was a multi-billion dollar business.

He raised a family of medieval proportions having over a dozen children with five wives. However, he focused his entire energy on his enterprise and had little time for being a good father. When he reached the age of seventy he decided to make all his children shareholders and divided the company between them, keeping only a small portion for himself. What he learned next was not a lesson out of Shakespeare's Richard III but rather out of King Lear.

Just as Lear learns that his erstwhile obedient and fawning daughters secretly held him in contempt and then actively undermined him after he divided his kingdom among them, so Shoen learns the same bitter lesson. His son Joe received backing from the majority of his siblings and staged a boardroom coup. Leonard was replaced as chairman by his son Sam, but this did not settle the leadership battle. The sons now in control did not prove able managers, and after being questioned sharply at a stockholders meeting actually came to blows in that forum.

To get away from the strife, Sam Shoen moved his family away from company headquarters in Phoenix to a small town in Colorado. His wife, Eva, was murdered one night by an intruder, and Sam and his father were convinced it was a contract killing to punish Sam who was backing his father in his suit to reclaim the company. After an extensive investigation no evidence of a contract killing was found. In 1999 at the age of eighty-three, Leonard Shoen drove his car into a utility pole in Las Vegas on a clear, bright day and died. The accident was classified as suicide.

Useful Lessons Learned for Boards, Practitioners and Those Who Would Be King

Selection decisions at this level require both art and science. Here are some best practices to consider.

For the Board of Directors:

- Have a shared definition of leadership. It is important to agree on what you're looking for.
- Resolve political and strategy differences in advance,
- Actively measure "soft" qualities in candidates and interview their subordinates for input.
- Be wary of candidates who act like CEOs and place undue emphasis on image.
- Know that real leaders can seem threatening—they bring change.
- Recognize that the current CEO may dread the loss of power and despise being reminded of his own mortality.
- While the CEO may want to choose his own successor for the sake of continuity, do not let this happen. Your obligation is to the future, not the past.
- Avoid using the entire board in the process. Form a selection committee of three to four members.
- Neglect external benchmarking at your peril. Find out what other, comparable companies are looking for in their candidates.
- Conversely, do not overvalue external candidates.
- Create a detailed plan for on-boarding the new CEO.
- Watch whom the new CEO selects for his staff. Does he favor weak or strong employees?
- Assess the new CEO early in his tenure with 360° feedback and personal coaches if necessary. Invest in his success and do not rush to judgment.
- Have a clear exit plan for the current CEO.

For Practitioners:

- Do not expect managers to be experts in developing people. Provide guidelines for assessment and competency training.
- People should not be rewarded or punished for results beyond their influence.
- No sense of accomplishment should be gained from merely completing succession charts. The real work is in development, tracking, assessment and selection.
- The IT system does not own succession planning. An over reliance on software is an abdication of responsibility.
- Formal management education programs, e.g., seminars, courses, retreats, on-line instruction, etc., are an overused approach for leadership development. Use job rotations and special projects instead.
- Management bonuses should be tied, in part, to developing others and self.
- Set specific goals for succession program, e.g., all key managers assigned a potential heir, replacements for any positions within a specified time, etc.

For Those Who Would Be King:

- As the heir apparent you should learn as much as possible about the current CEO, maintain regular communications with him, have a personal advice network and stay focused on the endgame. Do not get involved in petty squabbles that might display you to the board in a bad light. Derailment is possible.
- You may receive outside offers while waiting for promotion, and you may find them tempting if you believe your probability for actual promotion is low.
- "Poor people skills" is the number one reason for failure.
- If the firm starts performing poorly, outside directors may become reluctant to promote an internal heir for fear of continuing what is not

working. Seek to differentiate yourself from the current CEO in that circumstance.

- If an emergency arises regarding the current CEO, e.g., a medical crisis, the board may assign a board member with past CEO experience to serve until you are deemed ready. Persevere.

- Expect some to leave when you take charge. Some will feel passed over, others will believe they are about to be replaced with a new team, and others may disagree with the new direction you're taking.

- If you are perceived as a flawed choice, you will see a variety of reactions from your immediate staff. Some will try to protect you and provide coaching. Others will be very vocal regarding your perceived weaknesses. Still others will get in their foxholes and hide and wait. A final group will simply leave. This is why you must have some trusted advisors whom you respect and empower to be very direct with you.

The Battle of Bosworth and the Death of Richard

Just as a board of directors must evaluate a newly appointed CEO early in his tenure, so the critical factions evaluated Richard after his coronation. They were not pleased. Richard failed to build much needed support in the south, and while still maintaining his base in the less populous north, nevertheless suffered the burning enmity of the powerful Stanleys for his defense of the landed gentry against their avaricious quest for additional lands. Further, his reputation was blighted by the disappearance and assumed murder of the two young princes while under his protection.

Henry Tudor (later Henry VII) had a weak but clear genealogical link to the House of Lancaster. In the summer of 1485 he sailed with a force of two thousand men from France to southwest Wales. As he moved northward he gathered additional nobles, their armies and supplies.

Bosworth Field is approximately ninety miles northwest of London and is comprised of gently rolling hills, some marsh areas and level fields. At this site on August 22, 1485, Yorkist and Lancastrian forces would meet in a battle that would change history. On Richard's side stood about 10,000 men. These included 3,000 infantry with early cannon, 1,200 archers and 4,000 mounted.

Henry Tudor's forces numbered approximately 5,000 including 1,800 French mercenaries.

In a way, all of Richard's life had prepared him for this moment. His father, Richard, Duke of York, was adopted by Henry V, himself a warrior king, and although killed in battle when Richard III was only eight, taught him the importance of valor and courage. Richard's personal motto was "loyaulte me lie" or "loyalty binds me" and one of his favorite books was a 12th century romance about a perfect knight sacrificing for love entitled *Ipomedon*. To Richard, the "good old days" when men were men, and gallantry, chivalry and honor mattered, were three hundred years before.

Shakespeare captured his spirit when he imagined Richard addressing his troops a moment before the engagement:

> Conscience is but a word that cowards use,
> Devised at first to keep the strong in awe:
> Our strong arms be our conscience, swords our law.
> March on, join bravely, let us to't pell-mell
> If not to heaven, then hand in hand to hell.
>
> [King Richard III: V, iii]

The battle began with Richard's and Henry Tudor's forces exchanging cannon fire and salvos of arrows. Richard's supposed ally, the Earl of Northumberland, stood aloof with his army.

Richard decided to test Henry Tudor, who was inexperienced in warfare, and perhaps bring the battle to a swift close. He assembled a select unit of his mounted troops, arrayed them in a line facing his enemy, raised the standard, and led the last charge of knights in armor in English history.

They charged headlong across the sodden field with Richard aiming straight for Henry Tudor himself. Henry had a phalanx of guards protecting him headed by John Cheyne, a renowned jousting champion and a giant of a man. Richard closed on him with such stunning impact that he was unhorsed on the first pass. Then with sword, Richard killed Sir William Brandon, Henry's standard-bearer.

The phalanx closed around Henry to keep Richard away when William Stanley, who from the North Country was ostensibly allied with Richard, gave the order to attack him from the rear. Betrayed, Richard was cut down by the Welsh spearmen, fighting to the last. He was stripped naked, tied to the back of a horse and paraded about the field for all to see. From there he was taken to a local church where he was placed on display for two days and finally buried in an unmarked grave.

Afterwards, Henry Tudor married the daughter of Edward IV, Elizabeth of York (Richard's niece) uniting the two houses, and beginning the Tudor dynasty that brought forth Henry VIII and Elizabeth I. The Stanleys were awarded long coveted spectacular estates by Henry Tudor that were seized from supporters of Richard.

For a man who was king only two years, Richard left quite a legacy. Hugely talented and deeply flawed, he is mostly remembered for his ruthlessness and cunning. We easily categorize him as villain and turn the page. He was though, a loyal friend and a determined enemy—a romantic and a scoundrel—a knight and a knave. He was possessed of many contradictions and history will continue to judge and be confused by him. His lesson for us is that succession contests which degenerate into chaos that roils the countryside or corporation and engages the basest elements of our character, cannot serve us well.

References

Abbott, Jacob. *Richard III*. New York: Harper & Brothers, 1901.

Beiertz, Yvonne, et al. "Seven Succession Planning Missteps Boards Should Avoid." *Point Of View*. 2010.

Bennis, Warren, and O'Toole, James. "Don't Hire The Wrong CEO." *Harvard Business Review*. May 2000: 171-6.

Cannella, Albert, and Wei Shen. "So Close And Yet So Far: Promotion Versus Exit For CEO Heirs Apparent." *Academy of Management Journal*. 44.2 (2001): 252-270.

Clarke, Chris. "Succession Planning: Halt The Revolving Door." *The Corporate Board*. Jan 2008: 5-9.

Garman, Andrew, and Jeremy Glawe. "Succession Planning." *Consulting Psychology Journal: Practice and Research*. 56.2 (2004): 119-128.

Lansberg, Ivan. "The Tests of a Prince." *Harvard Business Review*. Sep 2007: 92-101.

Lee , Rowland V., dir. *Tower of London*. Perf. Basil Rathbone, Boris Karloff, and Vincent Price. 1939. Film.

Machiavelli, Niccolo. *The Prince*. New York: The New American Library, 1952.

Markham, Sir Clements E. *Richard III: His Life & Character* London: Smith, Elder & Company, 1906.

Miles, Stephen A. "Succession Planning: How Everyone Does It Wrong." *Forbes.com*. 30 Jul 2009.

Santora, Joseph C. "Passing the Baton: Does CEO Relay Succession Work Best?" *Academy of Management Executive*. 47.4 (2004).

Chapter 6

Creating Urgency for Change—The Day the Earth Stood Still

Upon its initial detection, ground-based radar operators worldwide were astonished at the sudden appearance of a huge, unidentified craft violating their nations' sovereign airspace. Its velocity was such that before any nations' defenses could react, it had traversed the borders of an adjacent country or soared over the great oceans.

Describing a perfect arc, its observed westward trajectory over the Atlantic indicated the dark green ovoid ship was heading toward Washington D.C., and on September 16th at 3:47 p.m. it landed. It had turned a public park in the nation's capital into its own landing zone, and those on the sun streaked ball fields, benches and paths had scattered in panic. A general alarm was raised and police and military units responded by surrounding the mysterious traveler with infantry and heavy weapons.

It sat for hours—motionless, silent. Barricades were placed keeping the media and curious back. Still it sat as the crowd grew restless and murmured endless speculations. Tank and artillery crews shifted in their seats; ranks of standing troops felt the weight of their helmets and rifles.

Almost imperceptibly at first, a seam appeared on the featureless metallic hull that silently spread in width and length to form a ramp to the ground. Anticipation and tension soared; weapons were cocked and then aimed as the strangely garbed humanoid descended. He raised his right hand in the universal sign of peaceful intent, but in that same instant a scowling robot, eight feet in height and constructed of the same metal as the ship, stepped onto the ramp. Such was the brooding presence of the robot that anyone seeing it was immediately convinced of its willingness and ability to defend its charge, and that it was not to be trifled with.

A panicked GI fired his service pistol and struck the space traveler in the shoulder knocking him to the ground. The giant robot reacted instantly, and with bursts of directed energy emanating from its cycloptic visored eye, destroyed all tanks and artillery pieces and disarmed all soldiers--without harming a soul. They had just shot Klaatu and been spanked by Gort.

Changing a World or a Corporation:
Is There A Felt Need?

Klaatu, (played by Michael Rennie) is rushed to the hospital and placed under tight security. He requests a meeting with the highest-level representative of the people and an assistant to the president visits his guarded hospital room. He proclaims that he has a message of the utmost importance for Earth and asks that an assemblage of all the world's leaders be arranged. He is rebuffed by the official and assured of the impossibility of bring together all the heads of state in a very divided world.

Regardless of the fact that this is the first encounter with any alien civilization, let alone a highly advanced one, officials don't see the need to oblige. Klaatu, in this role, is very much akin to a corporate CEO trying to gain the attention and cooperation of his employees. The 1951 science fiction classic

The Day The Earth Still has one overwhelming theme—the necessity of change for the sake of survival.

Organizations of all sorts are today in a constant state of change. Corporations, universities, and governmental institutions struggle daily with the need to adapt to a changing world and remain relevant and competitive. Typical change initiatives include:

- Quality improvement
- IT systems
- Culture/climate/leadership style/employee involvement
- Merger/acquisition
- Performance management
- Reorganization/restructuring
- Executive succession
- Productivity improvement/lean manufacturing
- Security systems
- Environmental/legal compliance

Yet, unless the organization as a whole accepts the need for change, which is often disruptive, the attempt is likely to fail. The popular estimate is that 70% of change efforts do not succeed. An example of national scope was the attempt to convert the American public to the metric system.

In 1975 congress passed the Metric Conversion Act and funded the U.S. Metric Board at the rate of $2 million per year. The concept was noble: The U.S. was one of a very few nations that had not converted, and for the benefit of international trade, standardization of measurements worldwide, and simplification to a system based on units of 10, it was the right thing to do. One problem—the people were not sold on it.

The change started in twenty states with metric highway signs, gas pumps and thermometers. Americans, however, did not like road signs in kilometers, gasoline in liters and Celsius temperatures. They demanded the return of familiar English units and began boycotting stores selling products sold in metric units including gas stations. Congressional efforts to force the system drew hostile and fearful responses. In 1982 President Reagan disbanded the U.S. Metric Board.

Industry has largely converted to the metric system to facilitate the multinational nature of production and commerce, but consumers are still offered products in English units. As long as food is sold in ounces and pounds, gasoline in gallons, and speed limits displayed in miles per hour, Americans will tolerate liters of soda and grams of fat. Just serve their beer in pints.

Alternative Tactics:
When Facing A Tough Audience

By the next day Klaatu's wound has healed and the physicians are dumbfounded. He escapes the confines of the hospital, acquires contemporary clothing and takes a room at a boarding house under an assumed name. There he befriends a young widow named Helen (Patricia Neal) and her son, Bobby. Aristocratic, handsome and urbane, he becomes a rival to Helen's boyfriend without even knowing it. From the other residents he learns that they are curious, fearful and skeptical when confronted with news reports of the extraterrestrial visitor. He reasons that since heads of state won't receive him, he had better seek out others of influence to make his case.

Klaatu learns of the renowned Professor Barnhart, (a.k.a. Einstein), makes his acquaintance and convinces him of his authenticity. He tells the professor that his mission to Earth was triggered by their recent observations of rudimentary forms of atomic power and experimentation with rockets. He warns that by threatening danger to other civilizations, Earth itself faces danger. They reason together that perhaps a demonstration of power might gain Klaatu the forum he seeks. Barnhart challenges Klaatu to devise a feat of stunning impact, yet one where no one is harmed. Klaatu, amused, accepts the challenge, and Barnhart agrees to schedule a gathering of the greatest scientists in the entire world at the landing site.

Dramatic demonstrations of intent and power have their place in organizations filled with skeptics and bystanders. In the late 1990's the Millstone Nuclear Power Station in Waterford, Connecticut was facing the combined threats of bankruptcy and investigation by the Nuclear Regulatory Commission (NRC). It was a plant of approximately 2000 employees that during the previous two decades had been viewed as an industry leader. A recent focus on costs, however, had changed things.

The NRC was receiving over fifty employee allegations per year in reference to backlogs in maintenance, serious problems in engineering and capital projects, delays in corrective actions and a generally unresponsive management team. The NRC placed Millstone on its watch list and ordered the company to show it was in regulatory compliance. Additionally, the NRC wanted Millstone to establish what it called a *Safety Conscious Work Environment*.

A new CEO, Bruce Kenyon, was hired and immediately brought all the employees together to describe his values of openness, honesty, two-way communications and high standards. He announced that he would perform a two-week assessment and then implement a plan of action. Further, he asked all his vice presidents and those one level beneath to grade their peers and comment upon their strengths and weaknesses. Employees remained skeptical during the review period.

After three weeks Kenyon made his move. Two of the three vice presidents were fired and the third was demoted. Forty managers were replaced, mainly due to poor people skills, and he launched an effort to take the pulse of the workforce through interviews and surveys. Finally, in an attempt to reduce fear among those reporting safety violations, he established a review board empowered to examine and approve all terminations. They started to believe.

The model for organizational change is often described as a multistaged initiative following a particular sequence:

1. A situation or condition is identified as in urgent need of change.
2. A new concept or vision for the future is crafted and communicated.
3. Key leaders are identified and selected to guide the process.
4. Actions are authorized and taken to implement the change.
5. The change is made permanent by ingraining it in policies, practices, systems and structures.

The model is by no means a static one, for the change process is often messy and does not necessarily follow a linear path. The single certain thing though, is that creating a sense of urgency requires drama.

A Shock to the System:
The Cure for Complacency

Two days after meeting with Professor Barnhart, at the stroke of noon on a bustling mid-week day in Washington D.C., the demonstration began. It began by stopping—everything. Electricity ceased to flow, period. Engines, motors of all descriptions, elevators, fans, subways and trains, clocks and traffic lights, drawbridges and bulldozers all ground to a halt. The phenomenon was not limited to the city. It was worldwide. The only merciful exceptions were planes in flight, hospitals and other such things upon which life depended. After one-half hour the power resumed.

Military and civilian authorities had previously noted Klaatu's escape from the hospital, but now instead of a curiosity, he was a menace. A frantic search was launched for him, and at the landing site the robot Gort was entombed in a super-strength plastic block. Attempts were made to penetrate the ship's hull with cutting torch and diamond drill, but the metal remained unblemished, and even attempts to locate the seam where the ramp appeared proved futile. They had been impressed by the demonstration, but did not conclude that they must now listen to his message, but rather that he was a threat.

Organizations can easily misinterpret inputs that signal the need to change. Even sophisticated and scientifically advanced teams, such as those found at NASA, can miss a harbinger of disaster. The Columbia tragedy is a case in point.

On January 16, 2003 the space shuttle Columbia was launched on the 113th shuttle mission. A little over a minute into the flight a piece of foam insulation broke off the external fuel tank and struck the leading edge of the left wing, damaging its ability to withstand reentry temperatures. Sixteen days later, at the conclusion of the mission, the Columbia disintegrated as it attempted to return home, killing the entire crew of seven.

Reaction within NASA was instantaneous and the Columbia Accident Investigation Board (CAIB) was established. Within seven months the thirteen-member board, with a staff of 120, issued a 4,000-page report with 29 specific changes to be made before the program could resume flights.

Portentously, over fourteen weeks before the Columbia launch, the space shuttle Atlantis experienced a significantly similar event. Slightly over one-half minute after launch on October 7, 2002 a piece of foam insulation broke off the external fuel tank and struck a ring holding the shuttle's left solid rocket booster to the external fuel tank. The Atlantis was able to complete its mission and return safely. A NASA Program Requirements Control Board ordered an investigation but determined that the foam strike was not serious enough to delay future shuttle flights. By the time of the Columbia's launch, the investigation had not been completed.

Organizations with long histories of success and achievement may be the most difficult types to convince of the necessity for change. Catastrophes that rock them to their cores are sometimes required.

Death and Resurrection:
The Vital Few

Military and police forces set up roadblocks throughout the city and were about to encircle Klaatu's boardinghouse when he escaped in a taxi with his confidant, Helen. He worries aloud what Gort might do if he is harmed, and he teaches Helen the words she must recite to the robot if he is killed or incapacitated. They are these: *Klaatu Barada Nikto.*

In an attempt to avoid capture prior to that evening's meeting with key scientists, Klaatu rushes from the taxi as the soldiers close in. He is shot in the back and dies. At the ship, the entombed Gort melts through the KL-93 super-strength plastic and does not disarm the two sentries on duty, but vaporizes them. Gort has been released to kill. Helen, terrified, confronts Gort and recites the order as taught. Gort's rampage is halted and it proceeds to retrieve Klaatu's body and return it to the ship. Once onboard, the robot applies astounding technology and resuscitates Klaatu so that he may address the gathering outside the ship.

What Klaatu is relying upon is his own ability to convince respected leaders in the scientific community of the urgent need for Earth to change, in ways he will specify, and that they in turn will be able to convince those at the highest levels of government. Klaatu is employing what has been called *Tipping Point Leadership* which holds that once a critical mass of influential people are engaged, fundamental change becomes irresistible and can occur quickly.

William Bratton, the highly successful New York City police commissioner, used such a strategy.

By the time Bratton received his appointment as police commissioner in 1994, he had already displayed his turnaround capabilities at four other troubled organizations: Boston Police District 4, the Massachusetts Bay Transit Authority, the Boston Metropolitan Police, and the New York Transit Police. In each case crime levels were unacceptable, morale was poor, and systems were inadequate or antiquated. In each case he left improvements that were dramatic and lasting.

The New York police commissioner assignment was especially daunting. With a budget of over $2 billion and 35,000 officers, the agency was beset with turf wars, funding problems, a negative culture, and most importantly crime rates so high that residents were fleeing the city to the relative safety of the suburbs. Only 37% of New Yorkers held a favorable opinion of the department.

Bratton had learned valuable lessons from his previous assignments. While in charge of the New York Transit Police, for example, he learned that none of the senior staff officers rode the subway. They were quite happy commuting in cars provided by the city. He changed all that for himself and all police officials. They began riding the subway instead of driving, and rode it for all purposes and at all hours. He forced them to experience the gangs, winos, beggars and homeless that ordinary riders endured.

As the new police commissioner, he decided to focus attention on those he identified as key influencers—the city's 76 precinct commanders. Each one directly managed 200 to 400 officers and he began mandatory, semiweekly strategy reviews that brought all of them together with his senior staff. In this high-pressure forum, a selected commander would be called before a panel of the senior staff and made to explain that precinct's performance. Accountability and goals became crystal clear, and precinct commanders introduced this same style of meeting to their own people. The change became irresistible.

At the end of two years the results were impressive: Murders fell by 50%, theft fell by 35%, felonies fell by 39% and the NYPD's approval rating climbed to 73%. New York had become the safest large city in the nation because Bratton had found the tipping point.

For Game Changers and Change Agents Only:
Do's and Don'ts:

DO:

- Effectively communicate need for change—repeatedly. Show why it's urgent.
- Invest in employees' technical and relational skills.
- Encourage participation that builds ownership.
- Link change support and effectiveness to reward system.
- Be flexible—change is not a step-by-step recipe, it's messy.
- Define success and describe what it will look like.
- Celebrate victories and analyze and learn from defeats.
- Express confidence.
- Answer employees when asked: "How will this affect me?"
- Help employees prepare for change so they feel able to cope.
- Survey workforce to determine types of change supported.
- Review progress regularly.
- Establish respected team to oversee implementation.
- Have supervisors involved in training and communication.
- Share information about customers and financial performance with employees.
- Expect poor earlier experiences to leave residue of resistance and skepticism.
- Change policies, practices, and procedures to anchor and imbed the change.
- Walk the talk—they're watching.

DON'T

- Confuse activity with results.
- Expect change to continue without strong leadership.
- Fail to hold people accountable.
- Endure procrastinators.
- Ignore resistance—it's feedback.
- Rush through employee engagement process.
- Excuse employees from pursuit of overall goals.

- Confuse participation in decision-making with need to control implementation.
- Ignore chance to learn from failure—analyze it and share wisdom.
- Fail to capitalize on external events to demonstrate need for change.
- Fail to set proper expectations.
- Ignore lower level managers.
- Flood organization with too many initiatives and create confusion and despair.
- Fail to consider amount of time it adds to current work.
- Give up.

Warning and Departure:
Change or Perish

By early evening, distinguished scientists from around the globe had gathered at the foot of the spacecraft. After a few tense moments the seamless metal skin opened and the ship silently deployed its ramp. Klaatu and Helen emerged followed by Gort. The crowd fell silent.

"...You will forgive me if I speak bluntly.... The threat of aggression anywhere, by any group can no longer be tolerated.... We have an organization for the mutual protection of all planets, and for the complete elimination of aggression."

"For our policemen we created a race of robots. Their function is to patrol the planets in spaceships like this one and preserve the peace. In matters of aggression we have given them absolute power over us. This power cannot be revoked. At the first sign of violence they act automatically against the aggressor. The penalty for provoking their action is too terrible to risk. The result is we live in peace without arms or armies, secure in the knowledge we are free from aggression and war."

"I came here to give you these facts. It is no concern of ours how you run your own planet. But if you threaten to extend your violence, this Earth of yours will be reduced to a burned out cinder. Your choice is simple: Join us and live in peace or pursue your present course and face obliteration. We shall be waiting for your answer. The decision rests with you."

The great ship's engines were engaged almost as soon as the ramp was drawn, and the assemblage scattered in a most undignified way as it soared into the night sky.

The same question posed to Earth is posed to all organizations concerned with survival and growth. Do you understand that change is necessary and urgent? Do you understand that without change there is no tomorrow? Are you willing to work for change, commit to change, and not stop until the transformation is complete?

A similar question then resonates in the mind of Klaatu and all leaders seeking change. Did I do enough? Do they understand? Did I reach them? What have I left undone? What will be their answer?

We know for a certainty that neither Klaatu nor urgently needed change will wait for long.

It may be hard for an egg to turn into a bird: it would be a jolly sight harder for it to learn to fly while remaining an egg. We are like eggs at present. And you cannot go on indefinitely being just an ordinary, decent egg. We must be hatched or go bad.

C. S. Lewis

References

Carroll, John S., and Sachi Hatakenaka. "Driving Organizational Change in the Midst of Crisis." *MIT Sloan Management Review*. Spring (2001): 70-9.

Jarrett, Michael. "The Seven Myths of Change Management." *Business Strategy Review*. 14.4 (2003): 22-9.

Kanter, Rosabeth M., et al. *The Challenge of Organizational Change*. New York: Macmillan, 1992.

Kim, W.Chan, and Renee Mauborgne. "Tipping Point Leadership." *Harvard Business Review*. Apr 2003: 60-9.

Kotter, John P. "Kill Complacency." *Fortune*. 134.3 (1996): 168-70.

Lawson, Emily, and Colin Price. "The psychology of change management." *McKinsey Quarterly*. Special Edition.4 (2003).

Lucey, John J. "Why Is The Failure Rate For Organisation Change So High?." *Management Services*. Winter 2008: 10-18.

Madsen, Peter M., and Vinit Desai. "Failing To Learn? The Effects of Failure and Success on Organizational Learning in the Global Orbital Launch Vehicle Industry." *Academy of Management Journal*. 53.3 (2010): 451-76. Print.

Todnem, Rune. "Organisational Change Management: A Critical Review." *Journal of Change Management*. 5.4 (2005): 369-80.

Wise, Robert, dir. *The Day The Earth Stood Still*. Michael Rennie, and . Patricia Neal. 1951. Film.

THE WOLF MAN

LON CHANEY JR.

EVELYN ANKERS

CLAUDE RAINS

A NIGHT MONSTER WITH THE BLOOD LUST OF A SAVAGE BEAST!

Directed by **GEORGE WAGGNER**   Associate Producer   **GEORGE WAGGNER**   **A UNIVERSAL PICTURE**

Chapter 7

Danger in the Workplace—
The Wolf Man

The scene is familiar: A lonely, darkened trail parting a desolate woodland of barren trees illuminated only by the cold rays of a full moon through contorted branches. A howl of astonishing power rends the still night air and strikes terror into the heart of a lone female trying to find her way. She quickens her pace, maintains composure, but can't help glancing over her shoulder at a presence felt but not seen.

We observe first the feet of her pursuer. They are neither human nor animal—heavily furred with padded, clawed toes, they move silently, briskly over the soft ground. The creature darts behind trees to remain concealed, though always closing the distance between itself and its prey.

She breaks into a panicked run to no avail. The beast seizes her, rips her throat out with powerful fangs, but then itself is dealt a deathblow from a silver-handled walking stick wielded by Lawrence Talbot, heir to the Talbot fortune. Before dying the beast manages to bite Talbot on the chest. The curse is passed, and the Wolf Man is born.

This 1941 classic, starring Lon Chaney, Jr. in the title role, laid down specific rules and conditions to which a proper werewolf had to abide. Primarily, the Autumn moon, (later any full moon) was his season, a pentagram would be present on some part of his body, that same five-pointed star, (that only he could see) would appear on his next victim, and his sole vulnerability was to silver.

The intriguing part of werewolf legend and lore is the requirement that a transformation take place--from ordinary to extraordinary, from man to monster. To the average person the werewolf in human form appears normal in every aspect. To the trained observer, however, there is the chance to see and understand the pentagram on his flesh and take action before it is too late.

Do we have that same opportunity in the workplace? Can we hope to identify those who may present a lethal threat to us before they transform?

Danger at Work:
The Werewolf Among Us

U.S. Department of Labor statistics for 2010 indicate among 4,547 fatalities in the workplace, approximately 11% or 506 were homicides. Four hundred and twelve men and ninety-four women were victimized.

Some fatal shootings at U.S. workplaces:

_ Aug. 3, 2010: Warehouse driver Omar Thornton shot and killed eight people before apparently committing suicide at a Manchester, Conn., beer distributorship.

_Feb. 12, 2010: Three biology professors were shot and killed and three other employees injured at the University of Alabama's Huntsville campus. Amy Bishop, a 42-year-old instructor and researcher at the school, is charged with murder.

_June 25, 2008: Wesley N. Higdon, 25, killed five workers, then himself, at Atlantis Plastics in Henderson, Ky. A sixth shooting victim survived.

_ March 18, 2008: Lee Isaac Bedwell Leeds, 31, shot and killed four men at a junk yard in Santa Maria, Calif.

_ March 12, 2008: Robert Lanham killed two people in the Regions Bank of McComb, Miss., where his ex-wife worked, then forced the woman to flee with him before killing her and committing suicide.

The FBI National Center for the Analysis of Violent Crime classifies workplace violence into four types:

Type 1 - Violent acts by criminals who have no other connection with the workplace, but enter to commit robbery or another crime.

Type 2 - Violence directed at employees by customers, clients, patients, students, inmates or any others for whom an organization provides services.

Type 3 - Violence against colleagues, supervisors or managers by a present or former employee.

Type 4 - Violence committed in the workplace by someone who doesn't work there but has a personal relationship with an employee—such as an abusive spouse or domestic partner.

Types 3 and 4 involve people in ongoing relationships of relatively long duration and are our primary concern. The werewolf knows its victim. In *The Wolf Man*, a foreboding poem is recited repeatedly:

Even a man who is pure in heart
and says his prayers by night
may become a wolf when the wolfbane blooms
and the autumn moon is bright.

Warning Signs:
The Pentagram

The table below divides the warnings into those external to the workplace and those internal to it, understanding that there may be considerable overlap. Not all signs need be present for the danger to be grave.

Internal	External
Threatens to cause harm. Makes unwelcome sexual comments. Makes suicidal references or plans known.	Bizarre or unusual conduct. Is withdrawn or a "loner." Prolonged depression. A sense of hopelessness. Dramatic changes in weight and appearance.
Angry, volatile conduct. Has a history of interpersonal conflict with co-workers. Co-workers fear him. Resists change. Monitors performance of other employees	Perceived persecution or victimization. Externalizes blame for disappointments. Feelings of humiliation. Paranoia. Will not accept responsibility.
Uncharacteristic attendance problems.	Excessive talk about weapons.
Lack of concern for personal safety. Disregards employer policies and procedures.	Family disputes or personal issues.
Excessive demands on managers' time. Threatens and attempts to manipulate. Files grievances with no merit.	Excessive financial difficulties.
Decreased productivity. Adverse reaction to criticism.	Obsessive actions or discussions. Fascination with reports of workplace violence.
Depends entirely on job for self-esteem. Unrealistic expectations of promotion, reward, recognition.	History of drug or alcohol use. Poor health, chronic pain.
Has been fired or laid off or fears that he will be. If fired, maintains contact with current employees—will not let go.	Has a history of violence toward women, children or animals. Has been arrested. Is known by local law enforcement.

Troubled employees who ultimately explode into frenzied violence may explain precisely what they intend to do, and how they intend to do it. This happens with remarkable frequency.

The Trigger:
"...the autumn moon is bright."

Oftentimes, a final event triggers the great unleashing. As Talbot is transformed by the full moon he experiences huge anxiety—he knows what is coming. Once transformed, though, he is an eager and skilled hunter.

Something akin happens to our workplace shooter. A singular moment, or sometimes the culmination of events, lead to lethal consequences. A termination, layoff or demotion, a corrective action or negative review, a feeling that harassment has reached an intolerable level, an affront to his dignity, or even the arrival of a critical date can be sufficient. Reaching a 10-year company anniversary, or the anniversary of a termination can also suffice.

Happenings external to the workplace are also effective. A bankruptcy, mortgage foreclosure, restraining order or custody hearing could provide an institutional trigger. Copycat killings are common, and historic trigger dates also obtain. The Oklahoma City bombing occurred on April 19, 1995 and killed 168 people. The Columbine High School shooting occurred April 20, 1999 and killed 12 students and 1 teacher. Adolf Hitler was born April 20, 1889. Is it coincidence, conspiracy, or conjecture?

If violence strikes, protect yourself. If you have an escape route, take it immediately and then:

- Call Security and local law enforcement.
- If no escape route is available:
  - Remain calm; in many cases your calm attitude can influence the person's behavior.
  - Never touch the person. Contact may increase the likelihood of violence.

- ○ Don't argue with the individual or antagonize him in any way.
- ○ Sympathize without being condescending.

Prevention, Preparation, Protection:
Your Silver Bullets and Amulets

In the movie, an old gypsy woman (played by Maria Ouspenskaya) gives Lawrence Talbot a protective amulet engraved with a pentagram to protect him from the curse. He, in turn, presents it to his girlfriend to protect her from him. What talismans can we use?

The first and best line of defense for your business is **a rigorous recruitment, interview and selection process.** If the danger can be kept outside the gates, all the better. It is far easier and less costly to eliminate a candidate before hire, than it is to rid a business of one afterwards.

Probing questions should be focused on what the candidate did in past positions, not what the candidate might do in a future position. Craft questions to explore:

- relationships with previous managers, co-workers
- achievements, failures, regrets, disappointments
- expectations for this position

If the responses tend to center on personality conflicts, blaming others, not being listened to, and unreasonable expectations, your antennas should be vibrating. Ask follow-up questions about reasons for leaving previous positions, especially if there were several of short duration.

Criminal background checks should be universally applied. Currently, over three-fourths of employers use them. Follow EEOC guidelines to avoid discrimination, and if there are convictions, consider the severity, number and relevance to the position as well as the length of time since the last.

Once the decision to hire has been made, the **on-boarding/orientation process** presents a key opportunity. Company rules and associated codes of conduct should be thoroughly reviewed. The new hires should have no doubt of the consequences for violations. Have them sign a document acknowledging the same.

Regardless of the date of hire, engage the new employee in your **performance management system.** Even if half or more of the current year is gone, assign goals and responsibilities to be met by year's end. In particular, stress the desired behaviors, (also known as competencies) that your organization wants to see demonstrated as the tasks are accomplished. It is another way to emphasize proper conduct, and it creates valuable documentation for future reference.

If it becomes apparent at some point, either because of a number of conduct issues that resist improvement, or a singular intolerable event, that the employment relationship must be terminated, do so with dispatch while maintaining the dignity of the employee. As Winston Churchill said, "When you have to kill a man, it costs nothing to be polite."

A few points to be mindful of:

- Do not argue or negotiate. This is not the trial; it is the execution.
- Choose a neutral, private meeting room or office. If the employee becomes argumentative, you will want to have the ability to walk out.
- Have security available but not present. Notify local law enforcement of the time.
- Decide if there are people who should be warned of this. The warning may prevent a disaster and protect your firm from legal problems. Keep the target separated from the potential perpetrator.
- Offer outplacement to keep the employee future focused.
- Advice on timing varies, but the end of the day or shift will give the employee the opportunity to gather his belongings unobserved by his peers and make a dignified exit.

Larger organizations may want to consider establishing a **Threat Management Team** (TMT) aimed at reducing the incidents of violence and equipping your firm with the ability to handle such an emergency. The team should include these elements:

- Build the core of the team around representatives from Human Resources, Security, Legal, and Medical (with special emphasis on your Employee Assistance Program (EAP)).
    - On an ad hoc basis include Communications, Public Relations, and Training.
- Train managers in the procedure for reporting threats or acts of violence.
- Develop a response plan for acts of violence, including pre-established contacts with law enforcement agencies.
- Designate an Incident Commander—the "go to" person.
- After a security investigation, hold a debriefing for the TMT for lessons learned.
- Require any employee, who has been removed from the workplace by reason of posing a threat, to be assessed as fit-for-duty before returning to work.
- Conduct management and employee training to raise awareness.

Avoid Self-Calming:
"You don't understand. You think I'm insane!"

Throughout the story Lawrence Talbot tries to convince the skeptics, including his father (Claude Rains) that werewolves are real and he presents a genuine danger. They, in turn, provide any number of excuses to him and each other as to why what he is saying cannot be true. They tell him he is exhausted, been through a shock after being bitten by the wolf, is in a "mental quagmire" and has succumbed to the "gibberish" the gypsy woman was preaching. He grasps reality. They have fallen victim to self-calming.

Self-calming is essentially a process by which thoughts or emotions that are uncomfortable are pushed aside. It takes place when we rationalize and justify actions or inactions by denying reality and favoring subjectivity. In its worst form it subjugates our survival responses.

Motivated bias is a close cousin. It occurs when people form and cling to false beliefs in spite of clear evidence to the contrary. It is a search for information that confirms what we already believe and dismisses information that does not.

After a workplace shooting has transpired, co-workers may come forward and remark how they always thought the shooter was strange or made them uncomfortable. For them to believe that their colleague was serious about committing murder, and then feel obligated to take the necessary steps to report their concerns, made them very uncomfortable and eager to dismiss their fears. They themselves did not want to be thought mad.

We are as well equipped as any living creature with instincts and a keen intuition designed to help us survive. We ignore that inner voice, that sense of unease, that prickly premonition at our own peril, as the employees at an Upstate New York textile firm found out long ago.

As reported in the Ancram Gazette, June 14, 1933:

Grizzly Murder Investigated At Local Business

By Jim Hart
staff writer

Workers at Taconic Fabrics yesterday were greeted by a horrid sight when entering the factory for the start of their 6:30 a.m. shift. Hank Jeffers, the night watchman who has guarded the business for the past seven years, was found brutally murdered.

Investigators are puzzled over a motive, as nothing was taken from the victim or the business. Sheriff's Deputy Norm Spears indicated there are no witnesses and few clues, though some employees did comment about a recently hired lift driver they considered "spooky." A special investigator from the FBI has been brought in to assist local law enforcement.

Investigators were examining what may be the only clues in the case. The FBI has taken castings of strange footprints leading away from the victim. The spacing between the footprints increases with distance, as though the perpetrator were accelerating with huge, lunging strides. The casting itself presents another fantastic peculiarity, for rather than the sole of a typical shoe or boot, there appears an indentation of four padded toes with claws two-inches deep.

References

De Becker, Gavin. *The Gift Of Fear*. New York: Random House, 1997.

Du Coudray, Chantal. *The Curse of the Werewolf*. London: I.B. Tauris & Company, 2006.

Lubit, Roy H. *Coping with Toxic Managers, Subordinates...and other difficult people*. Upper Saddle River, NJ: FT Press, 2004.

United States. Bureau of Labor Statistics, Department of Labor. *Number of fatal work injuries*. 2011.

Waggner, George, dir. *The Wolf Man*. Perf. Lon Chaney, and Claude Rains. 1941. Film.

INDEX

www.ingramcontent.com/pod-product-compliance
Lightning Source LLC
Chambersburg PA
CBHW051334170526
45166CB00002B/813